Clicker Basics
for Dogs & Puppies

By Carolyn Barney, CPTD

Clicker Basics for Dogs & Puppies

For information or quantity discounts contact:
Clean Run Productions, LLC
35 N. Chicopee St.
Chicopee, MA 01020
Phone: 413-532-1389 or 800-311-6503
Fax: 413-532-1590
Website: www.cleanrun.com

Edited by Marcille Ripperton, Nini Bloch, and Monica Percival
Book design and typesetting by Catherine Hawkes/Cat & Mouse
Cover design by Anne Cusolito
Illustrations by Catherine Fischer
Trademarks: All service marks, trademarks, and product names used in this publication belong to their respective holders.

First edition, 2007

ISBN 978-1-892694-16-4

Table of Contents

PART 1

General Guidelines

Welcome

This program is based on positive reinforcement using scientific theories. Training and behavior modification should be safe, enjoyable, and successful for both dogs and the people who love them.

This book will introduce you to clicker training, a very positive and fun approach to dog training. You will be guided through an eight-week, step-by-step basic training program. Depending on your time, dog, and ability the course may take you more or less time than the eight weeks. You can easily adapt the program to work at your own pace.

Ideally you should train on a daily basis. Use your everyday activities with your dog as training opportunities. If you integrate training into everyday life with your dog, it will be both easier to fit in and more effective. Consistency is very important when training dogs; therefore, all persons handling the dog should be aware of what is expected of the dog in each situation. If everyone handling the dog uses a different approach or has different expectations, the dog will be confused, and all will be frustrated with the lack of progress. Children in the household can and should be part of the training process, but only with adult supervision. Children should not be expected to be the sole trainer unless they are highly motivated and, in most cases, at least 12 years old; and even then they will need the support of other family members.

If possible, choose a primary trainer to monitor the dog's progress and do the bulk of the training. This will help you to achieve the most consistency possible. Keeping a journal of the dog's progress can be especially helpful if there are multiple trainers.

If You Are Attending a Class

The following are general guidelines that will help you get the most from your class experience. Do check with your instructor on policies pertaining to issues such as bringing family along to watch, equipment accepted in class, and makeup lessons.

Homework and Expectations

You are spending valuable time and money to train your dog. To be successful, you should attend each class and spend at least 30 to 60 minutes each day training your dog, breaking it up into shorter sessions for younger puppies. Use everyday activities like feeding time, taking a walk, and getting ready for bed as training opportunities. Ask your instructor for suggestions if you feel that you are unable to train as much as you'd like.

Mealtime—a great training opportunity.

Bring an Empty Dog to Class

You may want to skip your dog's meal just before attending class or feed him a smaller portion so that he is hungry and eager to work. Before class, please allow your dog to eliminate. Be sure to clean up and dispose of waste properly.

An empty, hungry dog will be more eager to work.

Training Equipment

Many dogs can be trained on a flat buckle collar. Be sure it is properly fitted and cannot slide over your dog's head when he is leashed. Other options, depending on each person's needs, include martingale collars, no-pull harnesses, and head collars.

Health Concerns

Please assess your dog's health each week before class. If your dog is vomiting, has diarrhea, is lethargic, or is coughing or sneezing, these are signs that he is not feeling well and should not go to class. Dogs contract contagious illnesses just as people do, and you should not expose other dogs. Another symptom to watch for is lameness or generalized pain or discomfort. Dogs can't tell you where it hurts, so you need to make sure that your dog is feeling up to attending class. When in doubt, always check with your vet. Be sure to ask your vet how long your dog will need to recuperate. Make your vet aware of the fact that you are attending training classes with a group and check with your vet before returning to the class environment.

Please also make sure that your dog is flea-free, and check for ticks during tick season. Make sure that you visit your vet annually for your dog's general well-being.

Bitches in Season

Check with your class instructor to see if bitches in season are allowed.

Top 10 Tips for Training in a Class

Here are my top 10 tips that will make you a terrific dog trainer! Following these tips will help you and your dog get the most out of this training program.

1. Be Consistent with the In-Class Trainer: When it comes to training, dogs thrive on consistency. Decide early on who is going to be the *adult* in-class handler, and then strive to stick with that handler for each week of the class. If you need to make a handler change, be sure to let your instructor know before class starts. While all family members can and should be involved with the home portion of the training, having a regular in-class handler will help your dog learn the exercises more quickly and easily. Check to see if the entire family is allowed to come to class each week and observe.

I recommend the in-class handler be over the age of 12 for safety reasons, or having an adult on the floor helping out. Be sure to check with your instructor before the class starts about age restrictions (if any) for a child as the primary trainer.

2. The Secrets to Success: Go to class and do your homework! Experience has shown that regular class attendance really does matter. Try to have perfect attendance for the entire eight weeks; your dog will thank you for it. Make time every day to work with your dog, even if it is only for a short session. Make it a fun part of your time together! Remember to *be patient* and help your dog along. Slow and steady progress with each exercise is our goal. While all dogs can learn at any age, the sooner you start training, the better. Make the most out of this once-in-a-lifetime opportunity with your dog!

3. Time: Be on time. Entering after class has already started is hard on both you and your dog. Late arrivals are also disruptive to your fellow classmates, so please make every effort to be on time for each class. Your punctuality is much appreciated by all concerned, both canine and human.

4. Questions: Your instructor will tell you when he or she is available for any questions that you may have. A busy class curriculum often prevents stopping class to answer unrelated questions "on the fly." Most instructors value your questions, however, and want to make sure your questions receive the time and attention they deserve. Ask for extra help if you need it; maybe a private lesson will help to resolve some issues.

5. Food: Training treats should be small (the size of a pea) and soft. You will need lots of them, and you will need to have them in a handy pouch or have big pockets that afford fast and easy access to the treats. Remember, do not feed your dog just before going to class; you want a hungry dog that is ready to work for you. When you are doing a lot of training, you may need to decrease the amount of regular food your dog is eating to prevent weight gain. This is especially true of small dogs.

6. Former Food: Make sure that your dog has had a chance to relieve himself before the start of class. Always have clean-up bags with you, just in case.

7. Your Training Equipment: As your dog's trainer, it is your responsibility to ensure that his collar and leash are kept in good repair and are fitted properly. See your instructor or assistant if you have any equipment problems.

8. Problems: Each dog is different and no class can address every problem a dog owner may encounter. Get together with your instructor to talk over any special concerns you may have regarding your dog's behavior. Some problems are best handled in a behavior consult that can tailor a custom-made solution to fit your dog and family situation.

9. Be a Team: Pay attention to your dog when training and make sure that your dog is paying attention to you—not wandering off to visit with his classmates. There may be time to visit with others before and after class; but during class, please keep your focus on your dog and your instructor. Be a team!

10. Relax and Have Fun: Take lots of deep breaths and keep smiling. Your dog is having a great time, so follow his example. Join in and keep it fun!

Practice—Here, There, and Everywhere

Students often observe that their dog performs the exercises perfectly at home but not elsewhere. This comment brings up the principle of generalization and how it affects your dog's ability to learn. To your dog, the environment in which the behavior happens is as much a factor as the verbal cue and the earned reward. Your dog thinks, "When I sit in the kitchen, I get a treat." So your dog sits in the kitchen. He does not generalize that behavior over to the living room unless you practice the sit exercise in the living room as well. So once a behavior is being freely offered in one environment, it is important that you then take the behavior "on the road" and practice here, there, and everywhere. Once your dog has practiced in enough differing situations he will generalize the behavior to most situations.

Practice in every room of your home, then in the back, front, and side yard. Practice in friends' and neighbors' homes and yards when possible. Stick to environments with few distractions at first, and then gradually increase the challenge by increasing the level of distraction.

Banks, schools, parks, post offices, video rental stores, playgrounds, soccer games, and even grocery stores present great locations in which to train. But above all, always make sure that you and your dog are safe from any vehicle traffic. Part of the reward of having a trained dog is that he gets to go more places with you! Use this goal to help your dog perform well everywhere you go. Always be on the lookout for training opportunities in new locations. New locales keep things interesting for you and your dog and teach him to remain under control in new situations.

Your trained dog will be a welcome guest at many events.

Need More Help?

If you are working on your own and are having problems with training, contact a professional in your area to get help. One good source is www.APDT.com, the website for the Association of Pet Dog Trainers. Look for a certified pet dog trainer in your area if you can find one. Get references and observe a class or lesson to be sure this is the right trainer for you.

Trained Dog, Happy Dog

Having a trained dog means having a happy dog that can enjoy many privileges. Trained dogs are well-mannered family members that are welcome almost anywhere. They are fun to be around and easy to take along on trips and family outings. A trained dog can be given the freedom to run in safe, supervised areas because he will come when called. Others can enjoy him because he doesn't jump on people. By spending a relatively short period of time training, you can have a dog that is a joy to be with for many years.

A trained dog can handle the chaos of a child's birthday party.

Solving Problems

Training not only helps your dog to be well-mannered and under control, it can solve most common behavior problems without the use of punishment. By teaching your dog the appropriate way to behave, you can praise him for being good instead of punishing him for being bad.

Some problems that training can solve include:

- *Jumping on people:* Most people do not enjoy being pounced on when entering your home, especially by a dog with muddy paws! Teaching your dog to do a sit-stay while being petted will enable your dog to enjoy company instead of being put away in another room.

- *Pulling on leash:* Dogs that pull on leash are not a pleasure to walk and tend not to get walked. Teaching your dog to walk politely on leash can help ensure that your dog gets enough exercise, which in turn may prevent many other problems.

- *Running away/not coming when called:* A dog that does not come when called is either unlikely to live long or will never enjoy a romp in the woods off leash. Trained dogs come when called.

- *Barking:* A dog can be trained to be quiet on command. Your dog is also less likely to bark and become a nuisance if you do some basic training for better communication overall. Training provides dogs with attention as well as physical and mental exercise, and gives your dog a job to do.
- *Chewing:* There are many reasons dogs chew. Among them are boredom, anxiety, and frustration. Training gives dogs mental and physical exercise to alleviate boredom, helps build confidence to quell anxiety, and provides an outlet for pent-up energy to relieve frustration.
- *Stealing:* The problem of stealing food and other items can be modified with training. Training will also establish trust. When your dog has something inappropriate, you can teach him to bring it to you and give it up instead of running away and destroying it.
- *Begging:* A trained dog can be taught to lie down and stay on his bed during family meals.
- *Biting:* Whether your dog bites out of protection, fear, or dominance, training should be part of the solution. Training will give you better control of your dog, will build confidence in a shy dog, and will help reduce the sense of responsibility in the protective or dominant dog. If your dog is biting, please get professional help.
- *Hyperactivity:* Overly active dogs are not fun to be around. Training helps you to control the hyperactive dog and allows him to use his excess energy constructively.

Training for Puppies

Training is essential for proper puppy development. By establishing communication and rules early on, you set the tone for a positive, constructive relationship and have a way to change or stop inappropriate behavior as soon as it appears. Training also helps housetraining go more smoothly and helps curb typical puppy behavior like biting, chewing, and jumping. You can start formal training when your puppy is eight weeks old.

The benefits of training your puppy or dog are countless. Your dog will be more content and under control, you will be able to enjoy your dog more, and you may just find yourself having fun in the process!

About This Training Program

Objectives

- To enhance communication between dog and owner
- To help develop your teaching skills
- To help your dog develop learning skills
- To build a harmonious human-canine family
- To develop a well-behaved, well-mannered family pet, leading to enjoyment of your dog-ownership experience and to a higher quality of life for everyone.

Behaviors

Behaviors are simply the things that dogs do. As dog owners, we need to put these known behaviors on cue so that we can manage them. By training, we teach our dogs to form an association between the verbal cue (such as the word, "Sit") and the desired behavior (your dog actually sitting on his bottom).

Behaviors taught in this program include:

- Sit
- Down
- Stay
- Come
- Let's Go (walk nicely on a leash)
- Leave It (leave things alone/turn away from things)
- Give (give me things you have in your mouth)
- Meet a strange dog
- Sit for greeting by a stranger

Our goal is not only to teach the behavior, but also to increase the reliability of the behavior. By reinforcing desirable behaviors, we help eliminate unwanted behaviors such as:

- Digging
- Barking
- Running
- Chasing
- Howling
- Jumping
- Sniffing
- Marking
- Hunting
- Exploring

We are not trying to take the dog out of your pup; we just want to gain some control over these behaviors by putting them on cue through training.

Getting the Behaviors that You Want

For your dog, there is a strong connection between information and motivation. You need to provide information about what behavior you want him to do and you also need to provide motivation for him to actually do what you've asked. Keep in mind that your dog works for rewards (his motivation) as do we (we work for our paychecks).

Therefore:

- Rewarded behaviors increase in frequency.
- Unrewarded behaviors decrease in frequency.

Keep in mind, though, that what the dog perceives as a reward might not be what you would think of as a reward. An example would be any physical reaction when a dog jumps on you. This reaction could be a reward for some dogs because it is attention. For some dogs any attention is a good thing. If you react to the dog's jumping up by pushing him away with the intention of punishing jumping, the dog might see this as a positive reward for jumping behavior.

Dogs learn the same way we do. They need information paired with motivation.

Some examples of information:

- Sound of clicker
- Verbal cues
- Hand signals and body language

Some examples of motivators:

- Food
- Toys
- Praise and/or petting
- Play
- Events (getting to go for a walk)

During our training exercises, the "click" sound (information) is paired with the food reward (motivation) and this pairing increases the repetition rate of the desired behavior. We begin by using a food lure three times at most for each training session. This will get your dog started. Clicking the behavior (or partial behavior) and rewarding the behavior with food will keep him going. Eventually, your dog will try different behaviors to get you to click so that he earns a reward.

A "clicker-savvy" dog will eagerly offer behaviors to earn rewards.

ABCs of Learning Theory: How Dogs Learn

Classical Conditioning

Remember Pavlov's dogs? During an experiment on digestion he found that when a bell was sounded and food was given right after the sound, after several repetitions the dogs would begin to salivate at the sound of the bell alone. *Classical conditioning* is when the bell became paired with the food that *followed*, and that combination then elicited the salivation. Classical conditioning is related to reflexes, not

Pavlov's dogs learned that a bell predicted food—just as a clicker predicts a reward.

to voluntary behaviors (for example, pairing food with a clicker or pairing food with a fearful situation to counter the fear). Examples of some human equivalents include the sight of a needle that produces a feeling of fear or the smell of dinner that makes you salivate.

Operant Conditioning

Operant conditioning is defined as "The part of [the] science of behavior that explains the functional relationship between environmental events and behavior. It is a key component in explaining how all organisms (including dogs) learn." (From *How Dogs Learn*, Burch & Bailey, 1999). In simple terms, what happens in the environment will affect what a dog will do in the future. If a dog receives a cookie for sitting, he will be more likely to sit again. If a bee stings a dog when he sits, he will be less likely to sit.

Dogs learn to counter-surf easily because the potential rewards are fabulous— it's a "high steaks" game.

Types of Reinforcement

Reinforcement is anything that will increase the likelihood of a behavior's happening in the future. To be effective, the reinforcement should closely follow the behavior to allow an association to be made. Reinforcers strengthen behavior.

- *Primary reinforcer:* Also known as an *unconditioned reinforcer*. A primary reinforcer will increase the likelihood that a behavior will be repeated in the future when it is presented immediately following a behavior. Primary reinforcers are related to basic needs: food, drink, and for some, touch.

- *Secondary reinforcer:* Also known as a *conditioned reinforcer*. By itself, a secondary reinforcer does not mean anything to the dog. But when paired with a primary reinforcer, the secondary then will also strengthen behaviors. For dogs these can include praise, the clicker, and petting. This pairing is classical conditioning.

There are two types of reinforcement used in dog training: positive (adding) and negative (taking away). Both types will strengthen or increase the frequency of a behavior. **This training program focuses on positive reinforcement and stays away from negative reinforcement.**

Positive reinforcement (adds something good)

> *Examples:* Primary—food, petting, exercise
> Secondary—praise, click, petting

Negative reinforcement (takes away something bad)

> *Examples:* Primary—stops tightening of the leash, stops delivering a shock, stops doing an ear pinch
> Secondary—stops a verbal reprimand or a sound, removes a threatening gesture

Note: Negative reinforcement is likely to have unwanted fallout and might shut down a dog's ability to learn. This negative reaction is why we do not generally recommend it.

Types of Punishment

Punishment decreases the likelihood of a behavior being repeated in the future.

To be effective punishment must closely follow the behavior. Punishment can be labeled positive and negative (just like reinforcement), and punishers also can weaken behavior. Although we strive to use as much positive reinforcement as possible, there are occasions when punishment is needed. Punishment should be used sparingly and thoughtfully, or not at all. When using punishment we usually focus on negative punishment, which can be a time-out of sorts. It has less fallout than positive punishment and is often more effective.

- *Primary punisher:* Also known as an *unconditioned punisher.* The dog does not need prior experience for this activity to be perceived as a punisher. Extreme heat or cold, a shock, a pinch, citronella spray, and hitting are all examples of primary punishers.
- *Secondary punisher:* Also known as a *conditioned punisher.* The secondary punisher only becomes a punisher when paired with a primary punisher. "No" is an example of a conditioned punisher when the word is paired with a primary punisher. For example you could say "No" then spray the dog with something he dislikes, such as water or citronella. The word "No" becomes the secondary punisher.

There are two types of punishment that can be used in dog training. Both types of punishment, positive (adding) and negative (taking away), will weaken or decrease the frequency of a behavior.

Positive punishment (adds something bad): **Use this punishment very sparingly and think through its use beforehand.** If the method you choose does not have an effect within three uses, you should rethink your plan.

> *Examples:* Primary—spray bottle, spray collar, leash correction, shock collar, ear pinch
> Secondary—verbal cue or sound just before the punisher

Negative punishment (takes away something good): **Works well and has little fallout for most dogs.** All emotion and anger must be left out of the time-out. You are simply removing the dog from the fun activity or removing the fun toy or reinforcer. You must be consistent; if there is a particular behavior you are trying to stop, you must use the negative punishment *every time* for the dog to understand. When you use this punishment, behavior interactions are over.

A time-out can be effective in stopping unwanted behavior.

> *Examples:* Primary—ending a play session abruptly for puppy biting, isolating in crate for time-out, removing toy, taking dog off an agility course for a broken stay
> Secondary—Verbal cue or sound just before removal

The ABCs of How This Works

A = Antecedent or a signal (cue)
B = Behavior (action)
C = Consequence (payoff)

Good consequence = Reinforcement (increases behavior)
Bad consequence = Punishment (decreases behavior)

Good Consequences Make Behaviors Happen

Human example:

A (antecedent or a signal): Alarm clock sounds (the cue to get up and go to work).

B (behavior): Go to work (the action).

C (consequence): Paycheck or payoff (you go to work for this). If your payoff did not happen, you would stop working.

Canine example:

A (antecedent or a signal): Trainer says *Sit* (cue).

B (behavior): Dog sits (action).

C (consequence): Dog earns reward (payoff).

Training Steps: B-C-A (Clicker Training)

When we are *teaching* behaviors to dogs, we change the order of A-B-C to B-C-A. We do this to maximize learning, increase the quality of the behavior, and improve stimulus control. *Stimulus control* is when a behavior is performed reliably on cue. The cue could be verbal or visual and should not be added until the behavior is happening reliably. Once you do begin to put a behavior under stimulus control you should stop rewarding that behavior when it is offered without a cue.

B (behavior): Get the dog to perform the desired behavior, for example, a sit. You could use shaping, capture, and/or luring (I'll explain these later).

C (consequence): Click and reward.

A (antecedent or a signal): Added only after the dog has become good at the behavior and will repeat it. When the signal is added, it is said or given (if non-verbal) just before the dog does the behavior.

By using the BCA order in dog training we are able to attach a cue (verbal or nonverbal) to a much more finished product. The dog is thus more likely to have a better performance of the cued behavior. For example, if you start by saying *Sit* and it then takes 10 seconds to get the dog into a sitting position, this 10-second lag can become part of the behavior. You could unintentionally be training your dog for a slow sit. On the other hand, if you teach a dog to sit quickly first and then add the cue as the dog is about to sit, the cue will be associated with a quick sit.

Clicker Training 101

The clicker is a secondary reinforcer. It is usually a small plastic box with a metal strip that makes a sharp, clicking sound when pushed and released. Its value is that the unique sound doesn't get lost in the babble of words we are constantly throwing at our dogs. It is faster than saying "Good dog!" and allows you to mark with great precision the behavior for which your dog is being reinforced. Paired with something he finds very rewarding, such as really good food (the primary reinforcer), the clicker becomes a powerful training tool. Taking advantage of this tool can help your dog learn more quickly. Using the clicker is like taking a snapshot of what your dog is doing and showing the snapshot to him! The clicker marks the behavior that you wish to increase.

Before using the clicker to train, you can click and then feed your dog to create the initial pairing of the clicker with food; we call this *charging* the clicker. Repeat until your dog starts to look for a treat as soon you click. When your dog looks for food after the click it means he has made an association (classical conditioning) and the clicker is now a meaningful secondary reinforcer.

You can muffle the sound of the clicker at first, especially if your dog is sound sensitive. If you know your dog is fearful of sounds, start by using the click of a ballpoint pen. You should reward every time you click.

Why Clicker Train?

- It's easy
- It's efficient
- It's effective
- It's educational
- It's enjoyable

Using a Verbal Click When You Don't Have Your Clicker in Hand

When you don't have your clicker you can use a verbal click such as "Yes." Any novel word will do, just keep it short. Either "Yes" or "Nice" is much better than "Oh, what a wonderful dog you are!" By the time you get the second word out, your dog may be doing something else and getting praised for the wrong response. I do not suggest selecting the word "Good" either because most of us say "Good" to our dogs countless times a day just because they exist and we love them. "Good" loses its impact as a reinforcer because it is diluted by overuse. To make the word you've chosen (for example, "Yes") into a verbal clicker just pair "Yes" with a food reward by saying "Yes" and immediately rewarding your dog with food. Repeat this as you did with the clicker. As with the regular click, reward your dog *every time* you say "Yes."

Training Games for Humans

Clicker training is a mechanical skill and is best practiced at first without your dog. Family members or a friend can help one another practice these skills. Help one another to watch for skill accuracy. Practice each exercise in 1-minute intervals.

Bean Games

1. *Treat delivery:* Practice reaching for a treat and placing it on a target (in a bowl or a hand). Using small dry beans works well for this practice.
2. *Neutral hand position:* Practice keeping your hand at your side or waist so it does not move toward the treat bag until you have already clicked. Click, reach, *then* feed. Practice just clicking, then reach for a bean and place it in a bowl or hand.
3. *Timing of click:* Practice clicking at the moment when someone moves a finger or touches something, or practice clicking to footfalls as someone walks. Try to click the movement, not after the movement. Better to be early than late with your clicks.

Human Shaping Game

Practice with a friend or family member. One person volunteers to be the trainee (a role usually performed by our dogs!), the other is the trainer. Use a clicker and candy. The trainer decides on a task and, using only the clicker and rewards, will get the trainee to do the chosen task without talking or pointing. Keep the tasks human and simple, such as touching an item in the room, picking something up, or sitting in a chair. Don't use tasks involving other people. The trainer should click when the person does something close to what is desired, perhaps just looking in the correct direction at first, just as you would shape a dog. Then hand the person a treat (candy in this case). Practice the mechanical skills of being still and not reaching or hovering over the reward when clicking, and of delivering the treat quickly but not before the click.

So how does it feel to be the trainee? And we know the game rules before we play; dogs do not!

Motivation

You must find what motivates your dog to be successful and make training fun and easy. One of the keys to motivation is introducing variety early on. Use everything your dog wants and likes, and use it in your favor! Use toys, a variety of food, play, walks, going outside, leash on, leash off, and so on. These can be very motivating objects or events to your dog, and they give you many opportunities to get the control you want in daily life. If you find what motivates your dog, the rest is easy! Spend time playing with your dog in a way he enjoys as long as it is safe. Tug is a great game for interacting one-on-one. Play is a good relationship builder and can be used as a motivator for many dogs.

For many dogs, splashing in the kiddie pool is a wonderful reward.

Choosing the Right Reward

Choosing the right reward for your dog is important. To discover your dog's choice of reward, complete the questionnaire below.

Does your dog like food treats? List his favorites:

Does your dog like to play with you? List ways that he enjoys playing with you:

Does your dog like to hear praise? List some praise words that he responds well to:

Does your dog like to be touched? List his favorite petting/scratching spots:

Get at least three to four different food treats (preferably soft, very small pieces) and two toys, spacing them out about 3' apart on the floor in a semicircle around your dog. Have your dog watch you do this with someone else holding him. Let him go, and then make a note of the order in which your dog chooses the treats and toys. Repeat the exercise a couple of times.

Finding a Good Food Treat for Your Dog

Just like you, your dog works for the rewards in life. As your dog becomes more and more skilled, you will be able to use less and less food, but let's get things off to a good start and use high-value treats for training!

Select a variety of treats that your dog enjoys. Let's first check out our local supermarket.

Question: What costs more per ounce, puppy-uppy treats or imported caviar? If you guessed puppy-uppy treats, you are correct. Check the price per pound and then read the label. Most dog treat labels read more like a can of paint than any food we would choose to give our dog. Why go to the effort of feeding a natural high-quality diet if we are then going to give our dog canine junk food? The supermarket is in fact the right place to be; we are just in the wrong aisle. Let's head for the deli and meat counter.

Here are some great dog treat suggestions:

- Cheese
- Chicken
- Hot dogs
- Roast beef
- Left over meat of any kind
- Liverwurst
- Homemade liver brownies
- Salmon
- Fruit
- Turkey
- Garlic steak
- Pizza crust
- Veggies
- Liver

When cutting up your dog treats, think small; the size of a pea is ample for most dogs; go much smaller for tiny dogs.

At this point, I must address the "people food" issue. When I go to the grocery store and buy people food for my dog, I intend to bring it home and cut it up for use as dog treats. There is a difference between making an informed decision to feed people food and simply tossing your dog some table scraps. Table scraps are leftover people food that gets reassigned to the category of "dog treat." Some table scraps may make acceptable treats, but be careful to use foods that can be easily cut up into small treats and that are easy to deliver to the dog.

Using small amounts of human-grade food as training treats is a fine concept that I hope you will strive to become comfortable with, since it will save you money and it is healthier for your dog.

There are also many high-quality dog treats on the market today. If time is a problem and you want to spend less prep time, look for soft, small natural treats. Read the labels and avoid things that are preserved with chemicals and those that contain artificial ingredients.

TRAINING NOTE   When training at home, kibble may work fine. Divide your dog's daily ration of kibble into two categories: what he gets in his bowl and what he earns from your hand. Hand feeding has the added value of teaching your dog how to be gentle when taking food from your hand. Use mealtime as a training opportunity.

Creating Fun and Rewarding Play for Both You and Your Dog

To your dog, it's all about play. At one moment he may be playing the chase-the-ball game, and then a moment later, the steal-the-laundry game. Later on, it's the bark-at-the-mailman game. By blurring the line between play and training, we can make teaching your dog more fun for all involved.

By playing with our dogs, we develop a better overall relationship with them. Some dogs are more playful than others, but all dogs will play to some degree. It's just a matter of finding the right game. It's amazing how many owners never play with their dogs. Know why dogs like children so much? It's because the kids play with them! Some of the best trainers are children, who really know how to use play to get their dog to do things.

Chase, fetch, tug, and hide-and-seek are all fun for a dog. Kong toys, Kongs on ropes, balls of all shapes and sizes, flying discs—all these are fun. For some dogs, food-loaded toys can create interest in play. Teaching your dog to catch, find, hold, give, tug, sniff, paw, bounce, balance, and nudge not only provides you with interactive play behaviors, but also develops skills that help you to train your dog.

Developing a strong relationship with your dog calls for exercising the relationship muscle, and playing is good exercise for both you and your dog. It not only helps you and your dog's physical state but also you and your dog's mental state. Boredom is a common cause of behavior problems in companion dogs and play is a great boredom buster. The number one reason people give for getting a dog is companionship, so make some time every day to play with your best friend. Remember, it's all fun and games to him!

Play is both a great bond-builder and a boredom-buster.

Praise, Praise, Praise

Verbal praise and encouragement are important training tools that can become wonderful rewards for your dog. Praise has the added value of always being available. Your dog loves to be told that he is "good" and you can use a praise word just as you use your clicker. Pick a short word like "Yes" and use it to punctuate good performances. Always reward your chosen word (yes, for example) as you would a click.

Strive to match your tone and excitement level to the personality of your dog and to the exercise you are training. Adopt a soothing and reassuring tone for the stay exercises, a happy and bouncy tone for walking on leash, and an excited and welcoming "Hurrah" for recalls.

Remember, if you want an enthusiastic performance from your dog, you need to be excited yourself and to praise him enthusiastically. Training needs to be fun for both you and your dog! Dogs seem to respond better to the higher ranges of voice, so if you have a deep voice, try to raise it an octave or two. If your dog gets overexcited, however, praise him in a quiet, soothing manner. If your dog seems a bit lethargic, be a cheerleader; get him excited and revved up.

> **TRAINING NOTE** Make sure that your dog's name is always a happy sound. Try not to turn it into a negative as in, "Rocky, bad dog!" If your dog is doing something that you dislike, instead of yelling his name, tell him "Stop!" or "Hey!" or better yet, use "Leave it!" Keep his name a sound that he loves to hear you say.

Touch Is Rewarding, Too

As humans, we love to hug and pat our pets. There is a place for physical petting in dog training as well; it is best used as a reward both after and between training exercises. Combined with verbal praise, treats, play, toys, and life rewards (see below), physical contact with the owner completes our canine-reward prize package.

Timing is important; physical contact while the exercise is in progress tends to distract most dogs. Physical contact interrupts learning. Imagine that you are studying for an exam or trying to learn a foreign language while someone is tickling you. A good phrase to remember while your dog is actually working is, "Don't just do something, stand there!"

Dogs respond to motion, so keeping your hands and body quiet while training can help your dog learn the verbal cue/behavior associations sooner. Once he performs the exercise, a well-earned scratch behind the ears or pat is certainly in order.

Dogs that need to watch their weight will benefit from having more play and touch rewards than treat rewards. You can also use meals as training rewards and decrease the amount of regular food when adding training treats to your dog's diet.

> **TRAINING NOTE** Gentle massage can help a stressed dog to relax in a new situation. When preparing to train in a new location, try giving your dog a gentle massage before you begin. It will relax both of you.

Life Rewards

Use life events that your dog enjoys as part of your reward system. Examples of life rewards include going outside, picking up his leash to go for a walk, putting the leash on, getting out of a confined space, playing with you or another dog, chasing a squirrel, digging, taking the leash off, meal delivery, and virtually anything that your dog perceives as fun. Taking advantage of life rewards helps to keep a high rate of reinforcement without the frequent use of food.

Starting Out with Your Dog

When you teach any new exercise to your dog, ideally start in a familiar, distraction-free environment. Distractions will be built in gradually to increase your dog's confidence and reliability.

Shaping Guidelines

Shaping a behavior (rewarding ever-closer approximations of a desired behavior) is the most powerful way to use clicker training. Here are some points to keep in mind as you are working with your dog.

- Have a plan! At each training session decide on which criterion you are working.
- Keep your hands and body quiet while your dog works. Click first, and then feed.
- Always ignore your dog's mistakes.
- Use a lure (use food or a toy to guide your dog into position). Each session lure at most three times to get the behavior started, whatever it is. Then wait until either a movement toward the behavior or the behavior itself occurs. Click and feed. Initially reward every behavior with a click and treat until your dog offers it often and does it well.
- Next, try letting the dog repeat the behavior twice before reinforcing with a click and a reward.
- Then begin to vary which responses get clicked and treated. Try to click the better ones, while still reinforcing often enough to keep the behavior happening.
- Don't attach a cue until the behavior is occurring consistently and correctly. This may take several sessions or several weeks or months, depending on many factors such as the dog, the trainer, and the complexity of the behavior.
- When adding a cue, get the behavior started (with a lure if needed) then wait for the behavior to happen. Click, then reward. When your dog offers the behavior with intent and at regular intervals of about 5 seconds or less, you can begin to add a cue word just before the behavior occurs.
- To put a behavior reliably on cue, stop reinforcing the behavior when it is offered unsolicited; this will teach your dog it is only worth doing the behavior on cue.

To help both you and your dog learn, practice shaping some random behaviors such as tricks. For example, place a safe but novel object (like a cardboard box) between you and your dog.

- Click the first thing that he does, such as touching the box with his nose, or pawing it, or, for some dogs, perhaps just looking at it.

- Say nothing. Continue to click anything your dog does with the box until he becomes very active with the box to get you to click and feed him. Do this for multiple, 1-minute sessions.

- Next try to get your dog to repeat one behavior with the box, such as just pawing. When your dog repeats that behavior, click, reward, and then wait for him to repeat the behavior again. Be patient! Click and then feed each time.

- As the behavior becomes stronger, try skipping a click to get two behaviors for the price of one.

- Name that behavior.

- Practice building new behaviors on the initial one. Ignore the pawing and try and get a nose touch or anything different. Repeat all the above steps.

- This repetition will improve your shaping skills and your dog's response to the game.

Rewarding your dog's interaction with a box teaches him to take the intiative and offer behaviors for treats.

Examples of How to Start Teaching *Sit* with the Clicker

You can use a combination of these methods:

- *Shape:* Start by using three lures during each training session (until you have attached a cue). Then begin clicking and rewarding any moves toward the behavior. Show the dog he can get a treat if something happens to transition from the lure to shaping. Click each full sit and try to get several repetitions during each training session once you are getting the full sit behavior. If your dog becomes distracted, show your dog a treat as a tease to keep him interested in working when you stop luring for that session. Be sure to use high-value rewards. If you don't get a complete sit as soon as you stop luring, start with clicking and feeding a head coming up or back legs bending: both can happen just before a sit and are precursors to a sit.

- *Capture/Wait:* Wait for your dog to sit unprompted and then click and feed. Confine both you and your dog with clicker and treats in a small room such as a bathroom so the dog might get bored and sit.

- *Target:* Teach your dog to touch and follow an object like a target stick or your hand, and use the target to encourage a sit by holding the target over your dog's head. Click and reward as your dog lowers his bottom to the floor.

Steps to Building a Reliable Response

One of the most important tenets of training is to *define your criteria.* This simply means: Know exactly what you want to reinforce for each training session. Have a picture in your mind of what you want before you start, and break down the steps you need to do to get to the end behavior. Work one element at a time. For example: if you want a straight, close sit in front, work on either straight or close, not both elements together in one session.

Expect your dog to make mistakes; this is part of learning. Ignore the mistakes and start the behavior over, pausing about 10 seconds between attempts. If necessary, go back a step in the training process. Don't use any negative tones or words, or even sigh for sensitive dogs; this can shut many dogs down quickly. If sensitive dogs think they are wrong, they will stop trying. If they stop trying, your training session is over.

When Training, Keep These Tips in Mind

- During the first few sessions, charge your clicker by simply clicking and treating your dog several times without asking your dog to do anything.

- Click *as* your dog is doing the behavior—the timing is important! Clicking a bit early is better than clicking late. Avoid clicking after the behavior. You are then clicking whatever the dog is doing at the time of the click.

- At first, click and reward each behavior every time it is offered. Be sure to always reward every click every time, always, even the accidental ones. Note: With two-fers (two behaviors for one reward), the click as well as the reward would be skipped for the first of the two behaviors; in this case you only click and reward the second behavior.

- Keep your hands in a neutral position when clicking, and then reach for the reward. Be sure that your treats are easily accessible. Do not place them in a baggie that could cause you to fumble when reaching into your treat pouch; empty the treats directly into the treat pouch.

Variable Reinforcement Basics or How to Get Away from the Food!

- You can be *variable* about *what* reward you give with each click. This is called varying the *value* of the reward or reinforcement: Cheerios to steak! If you clicked by mistake, use the Cheerio. If it was a breakthrough or if you are working with high-level distractions, use the steak.
- You can be *variable* about *when* you click/reward. Called *schedules of reinforcement*, this refers to the rules of operant conditioning pertaining to *how many* and *which* responses of a behavior are reinforced.

Building a Strong Response without Needing Food or Another Reward Present to Get It

Note: This information will be more or less important depending on what you need or want from your training. For the average dog you may not need to wean away from all reinforcement. If you intend to compete or need your dog to perform for a period of time without being able to reward him in any way, you will need to pay more attention to the schedules of reinforcement.

You can actually keep a rate of almost one-to-one (that is, one reinforcer for each response of a behavior) if you use all types of reinforcements available to you. Examples are food, toys, life rewards, petting, verbal praise, play, and so on. These will vary with each dog; for example, some dogs love petting, others do not; some love verbal praise, others do not. So unless you are in a situation such as an obedience competition where you cannot even talk to the dog during an exercise, you may not need to be as concerned about how often to reinforce as you are about what to use as a reinforcement.

You want to use a *variable ratio schedule* to build a reliable response when teaching behaviors to dogs. At first, the behavior is reinforced one-for-one to get the behavior to occur. As soon as possible, you want to get two-for-one (two responses for one reinforcer, such as two sits for one click/reward) and then work into a variable ratio schedule. Don't forget to add distractions and new locations at each of these levels.

For example, when teaching a Sit:

- At first click/feed every sit.

- Then click/feed every other sit (when not clicking, you should praise verbally).
- Then click/feed only the faster, straighter, better sits.
- Then click/feed only the perfect sits. (The trainer defines perfect!)
- Then you will click/feed the perfect sits on a random basis.
- Once your dog can do a perfect sit anywhere, continue to reinforce randomly (variable ratio schedule). Random reinforcement needs to be frequent enough to keep the behavior occurring between reinforcements. A sit probably won't take a high rate to maintain; however, something like a recall away from chasing squirrels will need a much higher rate of reinforcement to maintain the behavior. (You have to click/reward more often and use high-value rewards like chasing the squirrel as a reward for leaving the squirrel!)

Vary the value of the rewards with the effort. A sloppy down might earn a Cheerio; holding a sit-stay as a squirrel dashes by merits a hunk of steak.

Building Duration

To build duration you also need to be variable about when you click. You want to use a *variable duration schedule* for exercises such as stays, attention, and heeling. For example, when teaching a sit-stay, start with the initial behavior of a sit.

- At first, click/reward the dog's bottom touching the floor.
- Then wait until a few seconds pass before you click/reward; the dog is still sitting when you click.
- Then wait 5 seconds, then 10, then 6, 11, 7, 16, 20, 8, and so on. Vary the length of time that you wait, but slowly climb the ladder to maintaining a sit-stay for several minutes.
- Any time your dog gets up before a click, ignore it, pause a few seconds (not interacting with your dog), and then start the exercise over. Lower your criteria if your dog continues to have problems maintaining the sit before the click.

For more in-depth information on schedules of reinforcement see *Excel-erated Learning* by Pamela J. Reid, Ph.D. or *How Dogs Learn* by Mary Burch, Ph.D. and Jon Bailey, Ph.D.

Clicker Hints

- Practice makes perfect! Practice many (hundreds of) repetitions of each behavior.
- Train for 1-minute segments, stop, review what happened, reset criteria if necessary, begin to train again, and so on. By practicing this way you will have much more productive sessions in a shorter amount of time.
- Don't move toward the food until you click; doing so can distract the dog and weaken the connection between the click and the food.
- The more you teach your dog, the easier it gets. Your dog learns how to learn and you improve your skills and judgment. Practice by teaching tricks and "101 things to do with a cardboard box, a dog, and a clicker."
- Raise the stakes early on in shaping the behavior, but don't be afraid to lower them if needed, anywhere and anytime in the process. For example, if you skipped a click/reward too soon and your dog stops trying and is distracted, just show him the food again to remind him that there is a treat on offer. Do a couple more repetitions with reinforcement and try again for two in a row.
- Vary the rewards (the food, toys, and so on) to keep things interesting. The reward that is easiest for people is generally food, but it can be play, toys, getting to go out, meals, and so on. When using food, be sure to vary the food even for a dog that loves food. Vary means have at least three different foods in your bait pouch for the best attention. If you have a less-than-motivated dog, make sure he is hungry—that means training at mealtime for some. Set aside part of the meal for that day's training.
- The clicker is not a remote control! Don't use it to signal your dog. Use it to mark the behaviors that you want.
- Once your dog knows a behavior, you can stop using the clicker for that behavior. If you need to improve a behavior that is weakening then you can do a few sessions with the clicker to strengthen it again. Some call this putting "cookies in

A clicker is not a remote control. Don't try to use it to control your dog at distance.

the bank" that you can draw on for a period of time, using other rewards such as praise and life rewards between deposits.

A Little Help with Duration

To help extend a duration behavior, such as a stay, you can use quiet verbal praise and encouragement to let your dog know that he is doing the correct behavior and to keep doing it. This is where "Good" can come in! If, however, you need a solid stay with little or no encouragement such as for obedience competition then you will need to be careful that the behavior does not become dependent on your verbal encouragement by overdoing it.

Finishing Touches

Add distractions, vary the location, add verbal cues, hand signals, or both, and chain behaviors together. For example, put *Come* and *Sit* together to a come-and-sit-in-front-of-me whenever your dog is called, or you can try an automatic sit with loose-leash walking (when you stop walking, he sits automatically).

If you have further questions, here are some resources for more in-depth information:

- *Clicker Training For Dogs* by Karen Pryor
- *Don't Shoot the Dog* by Karen Pryor
- *Culture Clash* by Jean Donaldson
- *Excel-erated Learning* by Pamela J. Reid
- *How Dogs Learn* by Mary Burch and Jon Bailey
- *Clicker Training for Obedience* by Morgan Spector

Training Toolbox

Remember, your training toolbox includes:

- Collar and leash (Gentle Leader or a harness may be best for some dogs)
- Clicker, rewards, treat bag, and toys
- Lots of patience
- A good attitude
- Blanket, towel, or mat for the down exercise
- Dog food bowl
- Training workbook

Training Summary

- Be consistent.
- Keep it fun, upbeat, and positive.
- Don't train when you are feeling rushed, impatient, or angry.
- Plan to work with your dog for multiple, short practice sessions (3 to 5 minutes) each day.

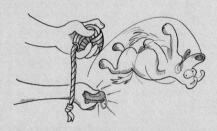

Keep training upbeat and fun.

Use mealtime, walks, and play as training opportunities.

- Make sure your dog gets proper exercise each day. If your dog is high-energy, be sure to exercise him before class so that you are training a slightly tired dog.
- Make sure that all your family members are involved in the training and that they are consistent in the methods used.
- Use your training throughout the day with your dog, not just in practice sessions. In fact, training works better when it's integrated into everyday life with your dog. Have your dog perform behaviors to get rewards; limit "freebies."
- Always practice in a safe area. Start with quiet areas with few or no distractions so that both of you can concentrate. If you own more than one dog, work with each dog separately.
- As your dog starts to learn the skill, start to add mild distractions (have other family members present, nearby dog toys, other pets, and so on).
- Always maintain your dog in accordance with local laws and use his training and your management to help him become a model canine good citizen in your community. When outside, always have a collar and I.D. tags on your dog. Identification that cannot be removed, such as a tattoo or microchip, is the best.

Terminology

As with any skill, there are terms used and it may be helpful to have a list of the terminology used when clicker training a dog.

Behavior	Something your dog does.
Click	A sound that marks the desired behavior.
Clicker	A small device that makes a clicking sound when pressed/released.
Operant conditioning	General learning theory: the immediate consequences of a behavior determine whether it will be repeated.
Cue	A voice command or a hand signal that begins a behavior.
Lure	Using food or a toy to guide your dog into a position, such as a sit or a down.
Jackpot	A big, unexpected payoff (giving your dog multiple treats all at once).
Shaping	Rewarding small approximations of a behavior and then raising the criteria until a final desired behavior is performed.
Stimulus	Anything your dog can perceive by sight, smell, touch, or sound. A stimulus provides information.
Reinforcer	Something that strengthens a behavior.
Response	A behavior offered in response to a stimulus.
Reward	Something pleasant that reinforces a behavior.
Fixed reinforcement schedule	Reinforcing a behavior on a predictable schedule.
Variable reinforcement schedule	Reinforcing a behavior on a random schedule.

PART 2

The Exercises

Some things to remember when training your dog:

- Patience—Remember, you are his teacher!
- Consistency—Everyone in your family must do things the same way all the time for your dog to learn.
- Practice makes perfect! Do lots of short sessions.
- Seek professional help if you are having difficulty and are not in a class situation.
- Motivating your dog will make training easy and quick. If you use the treat or reward that your dog wants, he will be more eager to do what you want—think of it as a paycheck of sorts. Use different levels of rewards, saving the good stuff for the challenging exercises or the times when your dog is most distracted. Also, remember that your dog cannot learn if you don't have his attention; you need to use rewards that will get his attention.

Week 1

Charging the Clicker

Your dog needs to associate the sound of the clicker with a food reward. To teach this, simply click and then reward, click/reward, click/reward, and so on. For the time being, food rewards should be close in time after the sound of the click. Do 5 to 10 click/rewards at the start of each training session this week. Be sure the click is first, then feed.

O.K.

Although the click ends the behavior, your dog may not always realize this. *O.K.* can be used as a release word at the end of every exercise. This way, your dog will understand that there is a starting point and an ending point to every exercise, and that you are the one who controls it.

When practicing sit, for example, if you click/reward and your dog remains sitting, make sure that you say *O.K.* in an upbeat, happy voice to let him know that you are finished with that exercise. *O.K.* indicates that it's time for another round of sits or that it's time to move on to a completely new exercise. If your dog tends to stay put even after you click and say *O.K,* try tossing his reward away from him after you click so that he has to get up and move to get his reward.

Alternative words are *Free* or *Break*. Your *O.K.* word can be anything you choose; pick one word and be consistent. Make the release fun to help increase motivation. If, however, you have a very excitable dog, release with a calm quiet voice and simply move him out of position.

Attention

The first thing you need to start training is your dog's attention. Begin in a quiet place with your dog on 3' to 6' of leash. *Wait* for your dog to look toward your face, and click/reward. If your dog is highly distracted you may have to shape the look to your face by starting to click/reward your dog for releasing the tension on the leash, flicking an ear in your direction, or making a quick eye movement toward you. Practice this for a minute or so when you start training sessions.

Targeting

With your clicker in one hand, hold the other hand with palm flat (fingers toward the floor works best) and facing your dog. As he touches your target hand with his nose, click/reward. Accidental touches count too! As he gets better at it, start to change the position of the target hand, waiting for your dog to move to the target each time. (Do not wave your hand about

You can use the targeting exercise to teach many skills that involve movement.

in front of your dog; just present the hand and hold it there until he touches it.) Each time your dog touches the target hand, click/reward. Keep in mind that the target should be held at a level that allows your dog to succeed. (For example, do not hold your hand above his head, forcing him to stand on his hind legs to reach it.)

You can also teach your dog to touch a target stick, which is especially useful for training small dogs. Get a dowel (a cylindrical stick that can be purchased at the hardware store for under a dollar) and wrap colored tape on one end to mark the touch spot. Have your clicker ready and your food nearby. Present the end of the dowel to your dog and click your dog's first investigation, trying to click the actual touch. Feed your dog and remove the dowel. Repeat this process, moving the dowel's location slightly each time, to the left, right, below, or above your dog's nose.

You will find as we progress that targeting is extremely useful in teaching your dog other new behaviors.

Do not say any cues this week.

Sit

Sit is a control exercise that is used for many purposes (for example, so your dog won't jump on you or your company). To get started, kneel down, sit in a chair, or stand with your dog attached to a 6' leash. Place the leash under your knees or your foot (with no tension on the leash). Hold three pieces of food in one hand and your clicker in the other. Touch your dog's nose with the food and lure up and back at an angle, holding the food just out of his reach until he follows the food into a sit. Click just as your dog's bottom touches the floor. Reward him with the piece of food. Repeat the lure twice, releasing each time after the click and reward. Next, show your dog a treat and then put it back in your bait bag or container and wait for your dog to move toward a sit. Watch for a lifting head or bending rear legs (if not all the way into a sit, a partial movement). Click and reward the movement each time, trying to get just a bit closer to the complete behavior with each attempt. Once you get a full sit, click and reward *each* sit. Practice in different areas of the house and yard. Practice multiple times a day for just a few minutes.

Do not say *Sit* this week.

Down

Another exercise that can eventually be used for longer periods of time (for example, during dinner) is the down. To get started, kneel down, sit in a chair, or stand in front of your dog. Place the leash under your knees or your foot (with no tension on the leash). Hold three pieces of food in one hand and your clicker in the other. With your dog sitting or standing (vary the position) touch your dog's nose with the food and lure him down (almost grazing his chest) toward his front feet and then out between his paws if he was sitting, forming an L-shaped motion. Click as your dog lies down. Reward him with one piece of food. Release your dog by saying *O.K.* and repeat the lure exercise twice. Then show your dog a piece of food and wait for a motion toward the down.

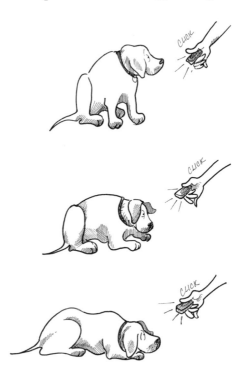

If he has difficulty going into a down position, click just when he lowers his head. Once he has been clicked and rewarded for that lowering motion, wait for him to go a little further down for the next click/reward. Break the exercise into smaller steps and be patient; keep your dog progressing in small enough increments for him to succeed. When shaping a down, look at the floor, not your dog, which will help prevent your dog's looking at you. Eventually, wait until he goes all the way into a down position.

Shape the down in progressive steps: First reward the lowered head, then the lowered front end, then the whole down. You can break it into even smaller steps.

Capturing the down is another way to practice the down. To do this simply click/reward your dog anytime he lies down even if you are not in a training session. If you do not have a clicker handy, say *Yes* and then reward just as you would a click.

Practice in different areas of the house and yard. Practice multiple times a day for just a few minutes.

Do not say *Down* this week.

Coming When Called (Recall)

Coming to you must *always* be a positive experience. Never call your dog to do something that he doesn't like, for example, clipping his nails, giving him a bath, or giving him a pill. Never chase your dog. Either he will love this game of chase, or he will become frightened. If you need your dog to come to you, you should crouch down, sit on the ground, or if your dog is in danger, run in the opposite direction to lure him away from the danger.

To practice recalls have a helper hold your dog a short distance from you, at first only 6' to 10' or so and always in an enclosed area. Call your dog's name to get his focus on you and as he heads toward you, click and praise him (saying "Good Boy" as he is coming to you, for example). Reward him with food when he gets to you and pet/praise/play with him. If you are working alone, call your dog's name from just a few feet away at first; as soon as your dog looks, click/reward. You can throw the reward away from you so your dog moves away and then you can repeat the process.

If he gets distracted and doesn't come when he hears his name, just walk up and put a piece of food on his nose, luring him back to where you called him from. Click and praise him as he comes with you, and reward and pet/praise him when you get to where you called him.

You can also play the Recall Game—calling your dog back and forth across the room between family members (each person has food and a clicker). If your dog is easily distracted, use a hallway to help him maintain focus. Practice 15 to 20 of these each day.

Do not say *Come* this week.

Sit-Stay

The sit-stay is an extension of the sit and can be used for longer and better control, again for problems such as jumping up. If your dog is sitting and staying, he is not doing other behaviors that you may not like!

Practice a sit-stay at each of his regular meals. Say nothing and lure your dog with his bowl of food into a sit. Begin lowering the bowl to the floor several feet away so it is not right under your dog's nose. If he gets up before the bowl touches the ground, pick up the bowl and lure him back into a sit (using the bowl, not your voice). Repeat this process until you are able to place the bowl on the floor without your dog getting up. Release him immediately at first (as soon as the bowl hits the ground, say O.K.). Each time you practice, increase the length of time you leave the bowl on the floor before releasing your dog. Build up to several seconds this week.

Once he is reliably staying, be variable about the length of time you wait before releasing him with *O.K.*

Do not say *Stay* this week.

Play with Your Dog!

Playing will probably reduce your blood pressure and stress level as you improve your relationship with your dog!

Here are some suggestions about how to get your dog interested in toys so you can use the toy as a means of reward and to build a better relationship through play. Please note that some dogs just don't seem interested in toys, but many can be taught how to have some fun, using a carefully selected object as a motivational toy.

Test a variety of toys of different materials, shapes, sounds, and general feel to see if something sparks an interest. If you have a food-motivated dog, look for a toy that holds food so you reward your dog from the toy. For a totally unmotivated dog start by playing with a closed bait bag.

Take a toy that you think may spark some interest and let your dog see you hide it in a drawer. Periodically (several times daily if possible) take the toy out and noisily and joyfully play with it by yourself. Become a kid again! As your dog becomes interested, give him a quick sniff of the toy and then play with the toy yourself and hide it away again. As your dog becomes increasingly interested in the toy, allow the play with your dog to go on for longer periods, always ending with your dog wanting more! Try to build the game into a game of tug, always maintaining a prompt response to a *Give* cue (see page 44). Reinforce the *Give* often with a treat to maintain it. Remember, you always win the tug game. "Winning" allows tug to be used as an outlet for energy and also for practice in relinquishing objects to you and maintaining a respectful relationship. Play can be a powerful reinforcement that can become even higher value than food rewards for many dogs.

For dogs reluctant to tug, encourage some retrieval of toys as a game. For those dogs that just can't get into play, there is always a good massage and belly rub!

You can also use your clicker to increase toy interest by clicking and rewarding any interest at all in a toy. Try to slowly shape the investigative behaviors of perhaps a nose or paw touch into a pick-up and then into a retrieve.

A Note About Playing Tug: While you are teaching your dog the tug rules, keep a leash on your dog to control the game. Try to use toys that are long enough to keep your hands safe. If your dog hits your hand with teeth, loudly yell "Ouch!" and end the game. Anytime your dog misses and gets your hand even by mistake (there are no mistakes allowed) the game is stopped. Ask him to *Give* often and unpredictably and reward the give with food or another game of tug. You always win and you always end the game, so quit before your dog does. When your dog will not release or trade for a treat, simply hold your dog by his collar or leash benignly next to your leg with one hand and hold the toy (but don't pull on it) with the other hand. *Wait* until the dog releases, praise and reward, and it's probably time to quit for a while. Practice more *Give* with clicks and rewards with many different objects to avoid object-release problems. See your instructor if the problem persists.

Once you have a playing/tugging dog, use play as a training reward in place of food sometimes.

Reminders

- Practice a little bit each day.
- Click, then feed—every click!
- Use really good treats.
- Play with your dog every day. Even 5 minutes of play can make a big difference in your relationship with your dog.
- Don't use any verbal cues this week.
- Remove your dog's training equipment when he is unattended.
- Make a motivational toy.
- If you are in a class, ask about convenient times to call your instructor if you need help during the week.
- Start using these training methods whenever you need to get control of your dog.

WEEK 1	Monday	Tuesday	Wednesday	Thursday	Friday	Saturday	Sunday	**Total**
Attention								
Targeting								
Sit								
Down								
Recall								
Sit-Stay								
Play with your Dog								

Score each exercise daily:

3 = He did great!
2 = He did pretty well.
1 = He didn't do very well.

Total at the end of the week:

15–21 = He's got it! Great job!
8–14 = He's getting it. Keep going!
0–7 = He's stuck. Ask for help.

Week 2

Attention

Work on your dog's attention in new places with increased distractions.

Targeting

This week, continue to practice hand targeting using both your left and right hand, and increase the distance your dog must move to touch the target. Take a few steps and have your dog follow your target hand as you walk.

Sit/Down

Follow training steps at your dog's pace. Practice in new places. No cues yet this week.

Coming When Called (Recall)

This week, continue to call your dog's name to get him to focus on you. Click as he comes toward you and praise him as you shuffle back a few steps. When he gets to you, reward him with food.

If he gets distracted and doesn't come when you call, just walk up and put a piece of food on his nose, luring him back to where you called him. Click/reward him when he gets back to the location where you called him from. Do 15 to 20 recalls per day, varying the situation, but always rewarding.

Continue playing the Recall Game—calling your dog back and forth across the room between family members if possible. Practice in new places with a long leash if needed.

Sit-Stay

Continue the food-bowl sit-stay at meals and increase the length of time before release. This week say "Stay" as you put down the food bowl.

Let's Go

Place your leash around your waist or through a belt loop. Begin with your dog's attention on you and then take just one step forward and click and reward. Repeat this one step until you have good attention from your dog and then try two steps between clicks and rewards.

Work for a few steps at a time and then release for a break. However, do not let your dog pull you around even when released. Never follow a pulling dog. This is very reinforcing to your dog and the pulling will persist.

- Always maintain a loose leash regardless of its length.
- Click and reward whenever your dog is walking beside you on a loose leash.
- A shorter leash will give a strong dog less leverage and will grant more control for the handler.

Do not allow your dog to pull on the leash to get where he wants to go. Stop and wait for him to release the tension before you walk again. This technique of stopping and waiting is especially helpful when you have no food. Your dog will learn that to move ahead, he has to maintain a loose leash. You can also stop and wait for him to loosen the leash, and then click/reward that behavior so that loosening the leash gains a reward. Practice both ways, with clicks/rewards for walking beside you and without them (by waiting for your dog to release the tension before continuing). Don't allow pulling on the leash to become a habit for your dog. If your dog is a persistent puller, back up a few steps every time your dog pulls you.

Pulling is a natural tendency so it is important to be very consistent and persistent! If the pulling isn't getting better, see your instructor for additional help.

Long Down on Mat

Sit in a chair and place a towel or mat next to you; lure your dog down on the mat, and click/reward him often while he remains in the down position. Release with O.K. after a few clicks and rewards if your dog does not get up on his own. Increase the length of the down gradually, by increasing the time between clicks. If he gets up, lure him back to a down position on the towel/mat, pause a couple of seconds, then click/reward with the lure; continue to click/reward quickly and often enough so the dog is staying down for a short period of time.

Door Safety

With your dog on a leash, teach him not to rush through doorways by gently closing the door if your dog tries to bolt when the door is opened. Practice *every time* you go through a door with your dog. Use your release word (O.K.) to indicate that he can proceed through the doorway.

If you choose, you can teach your dog to *sit* automatically at the door as you reach for the doorknob—as you reach for the door, lure once or twice into a sit. The act of sitting then gets you to open the door; however, your dog must wait for your release word before he goes through the door. If he gets up, simply close the door and repeat the exercise, waiting for your dog to sit before you open the door and release.

Keep your dog safe: Teach him to wait for a release to go through a doorway.

It doesn't take long before your dog figures out that to get you to open the door, he has to sit and wait. Be patient and consistent.

Play with Your Dog!

Keep working on play as described in last week's homework.

If you are not having any success talk with your instructor for some ideas and assessment of your dog and play.

Reminders

- Practice a little bit each day!
- Be consistent.
- Don't let your dog pull on his leash when you are out and about.
- Play with your dog every day. Even 5 minutes of play can make a big difference in your relationship with your dog.
- Use training in everyday life.
- Always have food treats available for rewards.
- Vary the locations where you practice.
- Refer to the section on "Puppy Biting" if you are having problems with nipping/biting during play and/or training.
- Have fun with your training!

WEEK 2	Monday	Tuesday	Wednesday	Thursday	Friday	Saturday	Sunday	**Total**
Attention								
Targeting								
Sit								
Down								
Recall								
Sit-Stay								
Let's Go								
Long Down on Mat								
Door Safety								

Score each exercise daily:

3 = He did great!
2 = He did pretty well.
1 = He didn't do very well.

Total at the end of the week:

15–21 = He's got it! Great job!
8–14 = He's getting it. Keep going!
0–7 = He's stuck. Ask for help.

Week 3

Attention

Just before the dog looks, begin to add a cue such as *Ready, Look, Watch,* or *Eyes Up.* Practice in more distracting locations.

Targeting

This week, continue to practice hand targeting, using both hands, and increase the distance your dog must move to follow the target. Say *Touch* just before he touches your hand or target stick.

Sit/Down

Practice in new places. Add distractions. Try for two-fers (two behaviors for one click/reward with a release between the two behaviors to get the dog up again). Reward the second behavior only. Begin to add the cue just before the dog is doing the behavior. See "Clicker 101" for shaping progression details.

Coming When Called (Recall)

Continue to practice as in weeks 1 and 2. Add new locations. Add the *Come* cue as long as the dog is responding well.

Sit-Stay

While working on duration exercises, begin to give your dog quiet verbal praise to increase the duration of the stay and to bridge the time between click/rewards. Smile, and say things like, "Nice Job!" or "Good!" or "Very Nice!" This verbal encouragement acts as a *keep-going signal* for your dog. Verbal encouragement is great for long stays. Be aware that verbal encouragement is not the same as a verbal click (*Yes!*).

You may occasionally feed in conjunction with verbal encouragement, but when you feed your dog, be sure that you remind him to *Stay* so he understands that he should continue the behavior. It is important for him to realize that the food does not mean that it is okay to get up.

Remember that the click marks the end of the behavior. If you do click, make sure to reward him. And if you click, you're telling him that the exercise is finished.

Be patient; this is a learning process for your dog and for you as well.

Let's Go

Continue to practice your *Let's Go* exercise this week.

Nothing tests your dog's leash manners like a taunting squirrel. If your dog pulls, stop until the leash is slack, then click, reward, and move on

Long Down on Mat

Sit in a chair, place your towel/mat next to you, and have your dog lie down on the mat.

Increase and vary the time between clicks gradually. While your dog is in the down-stay position, use verbal encouragement to maintain focus. Add the *Down* cue just before your dog lies down. And add a *Stay* cue if he is staying in position.

This week, try standing up from your chair. If your dog stays, click and reward. If your dog gets up, show him a treat and wait for him to go back into position, and then click and reward. At the end, release your dog with O.K. and step forward with lots of happy praise. Make sure that your dog gets up.

And remember, do not feed him after the release. You do not want to reward him for getting up. When you use your release word, O.K., do not feed, but you can pet, play, and praise.

Do five 1- to-3-minute down-stays with mild distractions each day. This week, work up to a 10-minute down-stay with no distractions.

Door Safety

Work on waiting or sitting when going through doorways and approaching stairways. Teach your dog to move out of your way when you need to pass through, so you are not stepping over your dog to get where you need to go. Gently shuffling your feet into your dog, using baby steps, and/or tossing a treat or toy to get him to move can accomplish this. As he moves, give a consistent cue word such as *Move* or *Excuse Me*.

Retrieve/Give

Get your dog interested in a ball or toy by tossing the toy toward a wall or giving it to your dog. Encourage him to get it, guide him back to you if needed, praise him, and trade food for the object. Click/reward, praise, and toss/give back the toy and repeat. When your dog begins to offer the object readily, you can add a cue word such as *Give* or *Drop It* as he releases it. Click/reward and praise.

When your dog steals things, *don't chase or punish him.* The act of having the object is a reward already. To chase him would be more reward, and punishing him after the fact won't stop the pick-up from happening next time. Trade a food or toy bribe for the object. Maintain a happy voice when encouraging your dog to give an object back. Try saying, "What have you got there, sweetie?" in a nice, happy tone instead of yelling, "Rocky! Give me that!" If trading does not work all the time, manage your dog carefully and pick up off-limits objects.

Always confine your dog when you are not watching him at this stage. If you are having any problems with aggression or possessiveness, see your instructor immediately because you may need additional help to prevent more serious problems.

Until your dog has a solid **Give** *command, negotiate for stolen objects.*

Leave It

With *Leave It* you teach your dog a cue to stop what he is doing. This exercise also teaches your dog the verbal click alternative (saying *Yes* in a happy voice each time and rewarding your dog so that you have a verbal substitute for those times when you do not have a clicker).

Start by holding a piece of food in each hand. Open one hand and as your dog goes for the reward, close your hand. Do not remove your hand or pull back. *Be sure* that your dog does not get the food. At the first hint of your dog turning/moving away from your hand, reward him with a verbal click (say *Yes*) and give him a reward from your *other* hand, not the hand he just left. Continue this process, switching hands occasionally, until your dog pulls away immediately. Once your dog moves away immediately add a *Leave It* cue as he moves away from the food.

Always be quick with the verbal click/reward during the learning process, and only use this command when you can control the situation (for now). Practice 15 to 20 times daily.

Reminders

- Vary your practice location three times this week.
- Never let your dog pull on leash.
- Use training whenever you need control: when company arrives, during meals, in the car, and so on.

- If you get stuck, back up a step.
- Use lots of verbal encouragement.
- Play with your dog every day. Even 5 minutes of play can make a big difference in your relationship with your dog.

WEEK 3	Monday	Tuesday	Wednesday	Thursday	Friday	Saturday	Sunday	Total
Attention								
Targeting								
Sit								
Down								
Recall								
Sit-Stay								
Let's Go								
Long Down on Mat								
Door Safety								
Retrieve/ Give								
Leave It								

Score each exercise daily:

3 = He did great!
2 = He did pretty well.
1 = He didn't do very well.

Total at the end of the week:

15–21 = He's got it! Great job!
8–14 = He's getting it. Keep going!
0–7 = He's stuck. Ask for help.

Week 4

Attention

Review your attenton homework and work on maintaining your dog's attention in new places. Use as a warm-up.

Targeting

Continue to practice with distractions and increase the distance the dog is required to follow the target hand or stick. Vary the distance.

Sit/Down

See the "Shaping Guidelines" on page 23. Ask for the behavior. Begin to randomize rewards when the response is consistent on cue. Add a *Stay* cue if you would like to, and add it when increasing the duration of sit. Increase duration by "ping-ponging" up and down within a set time of perhaps 30 seconds. Example: do a series of short stays, clicking and rewarding after 10 seconds, then 20, then 15, then 30 (if working on 30). Separately, click immediately for an instant sit on cue.

Recall

On leash, walk up to a distraction (person, toy, dog), back up (maintaining a loose leash), and call your dog's name *one time*. As he turns his head to look at you, say, *Come* and give a hand signal for him to come—your right arm outstretched to your side and motioning into your chest. Use food or toys to tease if you get no response; in this situation do not repeat *Come*.

Click and begin happy verbal praise as he starts approaching you. Shuffle back a few steps, and when your dog gets to you, place your hand in his collar and reward him, then motion him into a sit and click/reward for the sit.

You can sometimes jackpot your dog (give him a handful of treats, feeding them all at once). A jackpot will surprise your dog and may speed up his response. Continue to put your hand in his collar as you reward him with jackpots.

If your dog does not respond to his name, go to your dog, placing food under his nose, and lure him toward you using that food. As he follows, click and quickly shuffle back a few steps, motioning for him to sit, and reward him. Use the lure three times then wait for a response the next time. Repeat until your dog can leave each distraction immediately and then stop and have a play session. If your dog has a very difficult time, use less interesting distractions at first.

Do not use the verbal cue, *Come*, in a situation where you cannot control your dog and ensure his success. Practice off-leash recalls in your home and in a fenced yard when possible. Use a long line of 20' to 30' to increase distance, especially if no fenced area is available.

Be sure your dog can be successful; back up a few steps in your training progression if needed.

Let's Go

Practice in new places with distractions. Increase distance between clicks. Be consistent. Ask for help if you're not happy with your progress. Work on getting a sit when you stop. Cue the sit before you actually stop, wait for your dog to sit as needed, then click and reward the sit immediately. Sometimes release and play, and sometimes go back to *Let's Go*.

Long Down on Mat

Practice a long down daily. Sit in a chair and have your dog lie down at your side on a mat/towel. Use a *Stay* cue after the down cue. Click/reward if your dog remains in position. Begin to lengthen the time between clicks/rewards. Just start over if the dog gets up. This week, do one 15- to 30-minute long down, shorter for young puppies. Stand up as a distraction. Sit back down. Add other distractions when your dog can handle them.

When practicing the long down, begin to add distractions (such as you standing up).

Door Safety

Continue work on all safety exercises including doors and stairs, and make sure that your dog moves out of your way when you walk by.

Leave It

Once your dog is good at this exercise with food in hand(s), you should also practice with objects held or placed on the floor (but with a foot on the object to prevent him from taking it if he's too quick). Click as he turns toward you and reward him when he gets to you. Click/reward any turn of his head or any movement away from the object and toward you. If needed, use a food lure three times, and then wait for your dog to make any move away from the object and click. Be sure to practice with objects your dog particularly likes and with objects that are valuable such as remote controls, laundry, shoes, and eyeglasses! Use really good rewards. No cue this week for objects.

Gotcha

The purpose of this safety exercise is to teach your dog to accept your hand in his collar. This exercise is extremely important for your dog's safety and for the safety of anyone who may grab his collar in an emergency situation. Remember, never grab your dog by the collar in anger or frustration.

Sit on the floor, feeding your dog from one hand and reaching up with the other hand, placing it in his collar as you say *Gotcha* in a happy voice. As you repeat, move your hand faster, always saying *Gotcha* in a happy voice. This is a non-clicker exercise. Practice 20 *Gotchas* each day.

Reminders

- Practice a little bit each day.
- Add tougher distractions at home.
- Train in three new places and add more distractions.
- As you increase the level of distractions, make it easier: decrease distance; increase rate of rewards
- Do two-fers.
- Play with your dog. It is good for both of you!

WEEK 4	Monday	Tuesday	Wednesday	Thursday	Friday	Saturday	Sunday	**Total**
Attention								
Targeting								
Sit								
Down								
Recall								
Let's Go								
Long Down on Mat								
Door Safety								
Leave It								
Gotcha								

Score each exercise daily:

3 = He did great!
2 = He did pretty well.
1 = He didn't do very well.

Total at the end of the week:

15–21 = He's got it! Great job!
8–14 = He's getting it. Keep going!
0–7 = He's stuck. Ask for help.

Week 5

Attention

Review your attention homework and work on maintaining your dog's attention in new places. Use as a warm-up.

Sit/Down

Introduce hand signals for *Sit* and *Down* this week. These signals can be used for distance control (when you may not be heard) and when a verbal signal is not wanted, for example, when you are on the phone.

For Down: Signal with your right hand; raise your right hand, palm facing your dog, straight up above your head with the verbal cue given after the hand signal. Click/reward as your dog lies down. If he needs help, use a lure/tease in your left hand while holding the signal with the right.

For Sit: Start the signal with your right arm hanging at your side. Bend your arm at the elbow, bringing your forearm up, with your palm flat and facing up. Bring your hand forward until your forearm is parallel to the floor. Give the verbal sit cue directly after the hand signal. Use a lure in the right hand as you are signaling if needed for up to three repetitions. Click/reward as your dog sits.

Work on one hand signal then the other. Do 20 each per day.

Sit-Stay/Down-Stay

Sometimes use a verbal cue only, and sometimes use a hand signal with the verbal. When practicing the hand signal give the signal first then the verbal cue. Step in front of the dog when doing hand signals. Vary the length of time before you click/reward when working on duration. Begin to randomize your rewards to build reliability. To get better performance, reward only the better responses. See "Reinforcement Schedules" on page 26.

Recall

Practice with increasing distractions as your dog can handle them. See last week's homework for review.

On a loose leash, continue training your dog to come away from distractions, like a family member.

Let's Go

Increase time between clicks and increase distractions. Increase and vary the length of the sit when you stop.

Long Down on Mat

Also practice your long down daily for 5 minutes up to 30 minutes. Sit in a chair (during a meal is a great time to practice this exercise) and have your dog lie down at your side on a mat/towel. Praise verbally if your dog remains in position. Continue to lengthen the time between one click/reward and another, so they are further apart. If your dog gets up, place him back in a down on the mat/towel by restarting the exercise. Do a 30-minute long down-stay this week. If your dog is steady, occasionally get up and move around, staying in sight of your dog or try putting the mat a couple of feet away from your chair.

As a separate exercise, practice using a dog bed as a target. Stand close and wait for your dog to go to the mat/bed and lie down. You may need to shape going to the mat and lying down, clicking and rewarding putting feet on it first, and then reinforcing behaviors as they get closer to the down. Click and reward each response, occasionally taking small steps away as you are treating the dog to increase distance. Increase distance and duration at a distance slowly and separately. Try to build to 6' this week.

Leave It

Add a cue this week for leaving objects.

Gotcha

Vary your position when reaching for your dog. With one hand, reach for and put your hand in your dog's collar as you say *Gotcha* in a happy voice. Reward and repeat. As you repeat, move your hand faster, always saying *Gotcha* in a happy voice and rewarding. Do many repetitions per day.

Trick: Spin

Work on shaping a spin. Try using a hand target to get the behavior started instead of a lure. Use your right hand for spinning to the right and left hand for spinning to the left.

Sit-Stay for Petting

Use a sit as a means of preventing jumping up on people. Ask for a sit and stay before the person approaches your dog. If the dog gets up, the person stops or backs up and starts over. Repeat until a person can walk up to and pet your dog without his moving out of the sit-stay.

For extremely excitable dogs begin by clicking four feet on the floor. Then work toward a sit.

Reminders

- Click the better responses.
- Increase distractions as your dog can handle them and still be successful.
- Use better treats for better responses and harder situations.
- Work on generalizing behavior so your dog can follow cues anywhere: practice outside shopping centers, at kids' sports events, at the park, and so on.
- Your dog cannot generalize unless you train in a variety of locations during the learning process.
- Training is part of everyday life!

WEEK 5	Monday	Tuesday	Wednesday	Thursday	Friday	Saturday	Sunday	**Total**
Attention								
Sit/Down								
Sit-Stay								
Down-Stay								
Recall								
Let's Go								
Long Down on Mat								
Leave It								
Gotcha								
Trick: Spin								
Sit-Stay for Petting								

Score each exercise daily:

3 = He did great!
2 = He did pretty well.
1 = He didn't do very well.

Total at the end of the week:

15–21 = He's got it! Great job!
8–14 = He's getting it. Keep going!
0–7 = He's stuck. Ask for help.

Week 6

Attention

Review your attention homework and work on maintaining your dog's attention in new places. Use as a warm-up.

Sit-Stay/Down-Stay

Practice in new locations and with distractions. Use sits/downs as you need them in daily life with your dog. Reward randomly but often to keep your dog motivated throughout the learning phase. Use a higher rate if your dog is distracted. If the response to a cue begins to slow down, then you probably are not reinforcing often enough or with high-enough-value rewards for this stage in the training process. Vary the stay length of time and distance. Increase and vary distractions. Practice verbal only, hand signals only, and both together—mix it up to practice all.

Recall

Practice recalls in many different situations, off-leash in safe, fenced areas and with a long line. This week, practice a recall in conjunction with *Let's Go*. As your dog is walking on a loose leash beside you, stop and quickly back up for a moment as you call your dog to you. Try to get him to sit directly in front of you. Click/reward and then continue on your way.

Let's Go

Walk your dog toward something interesting to practice his loose-leash behavior of not pulling. If your dog is pulling, stop and wait, then click/reward a loose leash. Practice throwing in a recall by having your dog come and sit in front, facing you.

Long Down on Mat

Practice having your dog go to the mat and lie down, but with no duration at first. Do this by standing next to the mat and waiting for your dog to go to it and lie down. Click/reward. Be patient and start this with few or no distractions. Take a small step away and again wait for your dog to go to the mat. Click/reward. Allow your dog to come and get his reward so he has to leave you to get back to the mat; increase the distance another step and continue until you are about 10' away and your dog is going to the mat.

Can your dog do a long down on his mat with you 15' away, eating lunch?

Then do a 15- to 30-minute long down on the mat/towel. Reward occasionally while he is down, but don't lure him into position anymore. If your dog gets up, start over with one down cue and then wait; prevent escape by standing on the leash as needed.

Increase distractions. Move your dog further away from your chair. Try using this exercise during a snack or meal. Change one variable at a time.

Practice the targeting portion at first as a separate exercise several times a day if possible.

If your dog happens to fall asleep while he is in his long down, wake him up and say *O.K.* to release him when time is up.

Gotcha

This week after reviewing the collar *Gotcha*, begin to touch your dog all over. Touch first, then feed. This will accustom your dog to being handled all over and desensitize him to sudden movements toward him. Begin with slower movements and increase the intensity and speed as your dog can handle it. If you see any adverse reaction on your dog's part, slow down.

Trick: Spin

Continue shaping a spin to the right and to the left. When you attach a cue use a different cue for each direction. For left, the cue could be *Spin* and for right, *Twirl*. Add the verbal cue just before you give the hand cue.

Sit/Down

Continue to practice hand signals. Practice verbal-only cues, then only hand signals, and finally both together.

Sit-Stay for Petting

Continue to practice with new people and in new places. Vary where you stand, both next to your dog and in front of him. Make sure that all petting stops if your dog moves and resumes when he is sitting and staying. Begin to reward randomly if your dog is doing well with this exercise.

Your dog will earn brownie points for sitting politely as a stranger greets him.

Reminders

- Practice every day.
- Practice everywhere you go!
- Don't let your dog pull on his leash.

WEEK 6	Monday	Tuesday	Wednesday	Thursday	Friday	Saturday	Sunday	Total
Attention								
Sit-Stay/Down-Stay								
Recall								
Let's Go								
Long Down on Mat								
Gotcha								
Trick: Spin								
Sit/Down								
Sit-Stay for Petting								

Score each exercise daily:

3 = He did great!
2 = He did pretty well.
1 = He didn't do very well.

Total at the end of the week:

15–21 = He's got it! Great job!
8–14 = He's getting it. Keep going!
0–7 = He's stuck. Ask for help.

Week 7

Attention

Review your attention homework and work on maintaining your dog's attention in new places. Use as a warm-up.

Sit-Stay/Down-Stay

Practice sits/downs in new locations and with distractions. Use the behaviors as needed in daily life with your dog. Vary the length of time and distance for the stay. Increase and vary distractions. Practice verbal only, hand signals only, and both together. Mix it up to practice all. Continue to use random reinforcement. Use a higher rate of reinforcement if your dog is distracted.

Recall

Continue to practice recalls in many different situations and keep the level and quality of reinforcement very high. Reliability is extremely important in this exercise and requires lots of practice in many situations. Keep up your long-line practice in new places at least once or twice a week for continued success and improvement. Bring extra-good rewards for new places, which will be more distracting to your dog. Start with your dog closer to you if he has difficulty coming when new distractions are present. As your dog is successful, give him more line. Try to work up to a distance of 30', having your dog come to you without the aid of a lure or guidance.

Let's Go

Practice in new locations with varied distractions. Take your dog to shopping centers, town commons, pet stores, and any other place he is welcome to practice. Bring your treats and clicker and build a training session around errands when possible. Practice sits and recalls.

The pet store, with eye-level treats, is a challenge for loose-leash walking.

Long Down on Mat

Continue asking your dog to go to the mat to lie down in preparation for his long down. Practice using the bed as a target as a separate exercise several times a day if possible. Begin to add a cue that means "Go to your mat" once he reliably goes to the mat and lies down at a short distance. Examples of possible cues are *On Your Mat, Go Rest, Go Relax, Go To Bed, Bed,* or *Place.* This can then become your Go-to-your-mat cue (which means go to your mat, lie down, and stay until you are released).

Gotcha

Practice with both collar and body parts. Vary your approach and intensity. If your dog gets uneasy, slow down.

Trick: Spin

Continue to practice spin in both directions. If you have not already done so, begin to add a verbal cue just before you give the hand cue. Use one cue for one direction and a different cue for the other direction.

Sit-Stay for Petting

Continue to practice with new people and in new places. Vary where you stand in relation to your dog. If your dog moves,

Teaching Spin *is a good targeting and shaping exercise for both you and your dog.*

simply start over. Make sure that all petting stops if your dog moves and resumes when he is in a sit-stay. Reward randomly.

On-Leash Greeting

Try to find safe dogs to practice on-leash greetings with. Always be sure that other owners are confident that their dogs are safe with other dogs *when on leash.* Use caution to keep leashes from tangling and to *keep leashes loose.* This is important so your dogs can greet without the interference of body postures being artificially changed by the leash or by the owners' nervous tension telegraphed down the leash. Use the principles of cause and effect to maintain a loose leash on approach. To your dog, this means if you pull, we both stop; if you don't pull, our progress is steady. Be patient and persistent.

For particularly boisterous dogs, actually take a few steps backward for tight leashes if the pulling does not decrease with practice. Practice calling your dog away from the other dog by calling both dogs simultaneously, using a food or toy lure as needed to help the dogs come to the handlers. (Be careful using food and toys around dogs that may be possessive around other dogs.) This technique can be used for approaching people as well. End with a sit for petting.

Remember to *always* ask before allowing your dog to approach another dog on leash. Many dogs do not care for other dogs in their space. This aversion is especially true when dogs are confined to a leash and cannot leave if they choose to. Many dogs become more defensive on leash for self-protection or protection of their owners. If this is a problem, please talk with your instructor for further help.

If your dog acts aggressively toward another dog: Distract and feed him! Do not reprimand since it will only make the situation worse. Punishments will either increase your dog's fear or, from his perspective, show that you want to join in the aggressive behavior. Punishment after the fact does not work with dogs. If aggression is becoming even a minor problem, ask your instructor for recommendations, such as a consult and/or a different group class.

Reminders

- Praise every response; click/reward the better ones.
- Review areas where you need improvement.

WEEK 7	Monday	Tuesday	Wednesday	Thursday	Friday	Saturday	Sunday	**Total**
Attention								
Sit-Stay								
Down-Stay								
Recall								
Let's Go								
Long Down on Mat								
Gotcha								
Trick: Spin								
Sit-Stay for Petting								
On-Leash Greeting								

Score each exercise daily:

3 = He did great!
2 = He did pretty well.
1 = He didn't do very well.

Total at the end of the week:

15–21 = He's got it! Great job!
8–14 = He's getting it. Keep going!
0–7 = He's stuck. Ask for help.

Week 8

Attention

Review your attention homework and work on maintaining your dog's attention in new places. Use as a warm-up.

Sit-Stay/Down-Stay

Practice in new locations and with distractions. Use sits/downs/stays as you need them in daily life with your dog.

Recall

Create lots of distractions and go to new places to practice often. Once your dog is reliably (99.9%) coming on a long line of 30' or so, begin to drop the line when in safe areas and practice as you have been with a long line attached. If you need to stop your dog it is relatively easy to step on the line to stop escapes! If this happens you need to do more practice while holding the line. As your dog becomes reliable with a dropped line begin to reduce the length of the line until you no longer need one.

Please do not risk your dog's life or injury by allowing him off leash in unsafe areas because you think he is reliable. Off-leash is for safe places away from roads and other hazards to dogs. It only takes one squirrel at the wrong time, so use caution—even with a reliable dog.

Let's Go

Practice in new locations with varied distractions. Practice sits as you stop and recalls with a sit facing you.

Long Down on Mat

Continue to use the long down in various situations so your dog can do

An advanced application of the long down: your dog can maintain position with major distractions and no mat.

one in any situation eventually. Reward more often in more difficult situations.

Gotcha

Practice both body and collar *Gotchas* often. When your dog is very comfortable with your doing this, have all family members go through the same process.

Trick: Spin

Have your dog spin left and right, using your verbal cue for each.

Sit-Stay for Petting

Continue to practice with new people and in new places.

On-Leash Greeting

Continue working on your on-leash greetings. Remember to *always* ask before allowing your dog to approach another on leash.

Having a dog that is confident and calm about greeting other dogs on-leash means he can go more places with you.

Reminders

- Seek out distractions and new places to practice.
- Training is for your dog's entire life!
- Always look for ways to continue using your training skills.

WEEK 8	Monday	Tuesday	Wednesday	Thursday	Friday	Saturday	Sunday	**Total**
Attention								
Sit-Stay								
Down-Stay								
Recall								
Let's Go								
Long Down on Mat								
Gotcha								
Trick: Spin								
Sit-Stay for Petting								
On-Leash Greeting								

Score each exercise daily:

3 = He did great!
2 = He did pretty well.
1 = He didn't do very well.

Total at the end of the week:

15–21 = He's got it! Great job!
8–14 = He's getting it. Keep going!
0–7 = He's stuck. Ask for help.

Extras for Your Puppy

Handling

Teaching young puppies to accept handling is of great importance for general health exams by you, for going to the vet or groomer, and for general control. Here are several suggestions for handling and gentle restraint techniques:

- Hold your puppy in your arms close to your body and praise him when he is not struggling. Wait until he settles and then praise him quietly and release him. (For larger breeds, you may want to sit on the floor.)
- Cradle your puppy with your hands interlocked under his chest and elevate him slightly off the floor for 20 to 30 seconds. Quietly praise and release him when he is not struggling.

- Hold your puppy in your arms (or on the floor) upside down. Be gentle as you turn the puppy over so that you do not frighten him. The point is to have the puppy become comfortable with being handled and manipulated without becoming defensive. Belly rubs help with this particular exercise! If your pup is small enough, practice both in your arms and on the floor.

As always, wait until a struggling puppy settles before releasing him. It is important that you do not release a struggling puppy. If you do, the pup will learn that struggling works and he will use this as a means to get what he wants.

Children and Pups

A match made in heaven... sometimes. Proper interaction with children includes never leaving children alone with puppies or dogs. Pups view children as littermates and will often compete and play roughly with them. Children's quick movements and higher-pitched voices also tend to excite puppies and dogs. This excitement can lead to very serious problems as the pup matures. Small children and puppies always need to be monitored and often need to be separated. Include your children in your training. Have them do some of the lure training or have them give the food reward after you click. Older children are often very good at clicker training and can share in the training time.

Please note that it is unfair to expect most children to do the bulk of the training until they are at least 12 years old and even then, they will need an adult to help them.

If you do not have children of your own, try to find some children that you can acquaint your young puppy with in a positive manner. Ideally, introduce puppies to well-mannered children in a controlled setting before the puppy is 16 weeks old; before 12 weeks is even better. Most puppies gravitate toward children and vice versa. However, it is important that an adult carefully monitors this interaction to be sure that it is a positive experience for the puppy. Watch for any signs of fearfulness. (Handle fear as described in the section called "Fearful Pups and Dogs" on page 67.)

Teething

Pups teethe just like babies; this is one reason why puppies chew. It is important to teach appropriate versus inappropriate chewing. Confine your pup to *prevent* inappropriate chewing when you cannot *watch him* 100% of the time. Praise your puppy when he has chosen appropriate toys to chew on. A chewed possession is never the fault of the puppy. When you catch him with an inappropriate object, *quietly* ask him for it by trading for a toy or food reward. Give him an appropriate chew toy as a replacement. Blame yourself, not the pup, for ruined items.

For pups, toy variety is the spice of life and helps prevent boredom, frustration, and destructive chewing.

Toys, Bones, and Food Bowls

Have a variety of hard and soft, safe chew toys available. Rotate the toys that are left out so that they are more interesting. Give your pup at most three to four toys at any one time. Sometimes, take a toy away happily and give it right back. Occasionally pick up your pup's food dish to *add* more food; don't overdo, and make it positive. *If your puppy is protective of the dish, add food at first without picking it up.*

Never allow children to take toys or food from the pup when unsupervised. If you are having problems with any sort of possessiveness, please seek professional help immediately. This is a problem that needs to be dealt with positively, carefully, and quickly.

Puppy Biting

Puppies use their mouths to explore their environment and to learn about being a dog. They must bite in order to learn bite inhibition. Bite inhibition is the ability to control the amount of pressure used while biting. It is one of the most important lessons a young puppy can learn.

The needle sharp puppy teeth have only one purpose—to hurt what they are used on! Initially, when still nursing, they learn from mom not to bite down. She teaches them this through a menacing look at first, followed by a growl if they don't respond, and when that doesn't work, she will "tag" them with her mouth but will not do damage. This begins the process of bite inhibition, which is continued through play with littermates. When one pup bites too hard, the other one yelps and the biter stops. These lessons with mom and littermates are crucial to a dog's behaving normally as an adult and should continue until eight weeks of age. Puppies should not be separated from their mother or littermates before this age. Unfortunately, this is not always the case and it will take more work on the owners' part to teach bite inhibition, but it can be done. Puppies taken away too early must be socialized through other avenues, such as puppy classes and carefully monitored playgroups. All puppies will benefit from this interaction, even if they were with mom and littermates for the full eight weeks.

How to Handle Puppy Biting

Puppies up to 11 or 12 weeks need to continue to learn bite inhibition. When they mouth you hard enough to cause discomfort, yelp with a high-pitched "Ouch!" Most puppies will immediately stop (at least for a moment). Have a toy handy and encourage the puppy to bite the toy instead. If your puppy persists in biting you, yelp, and leave the room. This ends the attention/play, which is not what the puppy wanted. He will eventually associate his biting with your leaving—and this is no fun. When needed, to control the situation, place the puppy in a time-out in his crate or in a confined area. There should be no scolding or punishment associated with the time-out, just the end of attention from you.

Puppies over the age of 12 weeks should begin to learn not to put their mouth on a human. To teach this, modify the above lesson by leaving immediately or by placing the puppy in a time-out immediately upon biting. Skip the "Ouch!" The play should end as soon as his mouth touches you. Continue to use toys and chew bones to encourage proper play with people. (Toys go in your mouth, not human parts!) Puppies and dogs learn quickly when what they want goes away or when play ends, and they can learn to control their environment through appropriate actions. We all win when we use this concept in their training.

Puppies should also be on a high-quality premium diet with no preservatives. If the pup is not getting proper or optimal nutrition, this can make common puppy problems like chewing or housebreaking worse. Avoid chemical preservatives, dyes, sugar additives, and diets that are mostly grain or have high-grain content. Dogs are primarily carnivores and do best on a diet that is properly balanced and made mostly of animal product. Be sure that your puppy is getting enough exercise every day.

Train your puppy using positive methods, and use them throughout the day, not just during a training session. This way, training becomes part of everyday life. The investment of energy you put into your puppy during the first year will pay off for the next 10 to 15 years, or longer if you're lucky!

If you have tried these suggestions and are not happy with your progress, seek professional help.

PART 3

Dealing with Common Problems

There are several common problems you may be concerned about. This section deals with some specific behaviors and how you can cope with them.

Fearful Pups and Dogs

General Fear Issues

Puppies and dogs go through a variety of critical periods during their developmental stages. Some of those critical periods are times when fearful situations will have a stronger impact. At about 8 to 11 weeks of age, the first fear-imprint period will occur. You may or may not notice anything different in your pup's behavior. Some pups will tend to be more cautious of a new stimulus presented to them. Others will not show any signs of change. During this time, avoid situations that may be particularly scary or over-whelming to a puppy and certainly monitor their reac-

You can help your dog overcome fearful reactions.

tions to new situations and be ready to boost their confidence. An example of something to avoid would be elective surgery. Examples of where to keep a watchful eye are new situations and meeting new people and dogs; however, these are things that you must be doing with a puppy of this age for normal social development, so just watch for your puppy's reaction in these situations.

Regardless of age, if your pup or dog is afraid of something or someone, approach the object of fear yourself *without forcing the pup* to go with you. Talk silly to the object or person. Touch it, and gently encourage the pup to approach it. At no time should the leash become tight. Always allow a dog to leave a frightening situation, go to a distance where he can tolerate it, and then begin to work toward getting him closer, but always on his own terms. Click and reward each step toward a scary object or person—it should *always* be the dog's choice to move forward and he should always be allowed to move away.

Fear of People

When your puppy or dog is afraid of a person, it is very important that the person follows your instructions. If they will not or cannot, it is your responsibility to remove your dog from that situation so that no further damage is done. Beware of the person who says, "All dogs love me." These people are often a target for pushing a dog to bite out of self-defense. Dogs learn from experience. If they are afraid, and what they are afraid of is forced on them, their fear will increase. The next time a similar situation arises, the dog's reaction will increase and it will take longer to repair the damage. As with other situations, it must always be the dog that makes the move, not the person.

The best way to handle fear of people is to have people ignore the dog completely. The scary person should be supplied with really good food treats and get into a non-threatening position (the person can either sit in a chair or with smaller safer dogs, the person can sit on the floor). The scary person should sit sideways to the dog, not directly facing him. The person should ignore the dog unless the dog approaches. When the dog approaches, depending on the level of fear, the person can offer a treat by dropping it on the floor or holding his hand out, palm flat, with food on it. You should generally just ignore the dog and talk quietly with the person so that the dog sees normal interactions.

It will depend on the dog's level of fear and past experiences (or lack thereof) as to how long it will take to overcome his fears. If you are concerned about the level of fear your dog exhibits, please speak with a professional to determine if further help is needed or if you should just allow more time.

Classical Counterconditioning

Reward *without* clicking for being in the vicinity of a scary person or object. Work at a tolerable distance for your dog. The dog should readily take a treat. If your dog will not take a treat you need to back away to a distance where he can, then you can move closer. Once your dog begins to ignore the object or person, you can ask for behaviors that you can then click and reward, such as a sit. Next move closer and start over. By doing this slowly and systematically you may be able to overcome some fear issues. Go very slowly.

Fear and Vet Visits

To help make a vet visit a pleasant experience, bring food and toys to distract your pup from the scary things at the vet (like needles!). Avoid elective surgery between 8 and 11 weeks.

Solving Destructive Chewing

Destructive chewing is one of the most common complaints among dog owners. It can be a frustrating problem—and an expensive one. Chewing is not bad. It is a normal and necessary activity for a dog. Chewing only becomes a problem when your dog chews things you don't want him to chew. This information is designed to help you understand why your dog is being destructive and to offer you some avenues toward a solution.

"He Ate the Couch Because He's Mad at Me."

Your dog may chew for any number of reasons, but among those reasons anger, spite, or hatred has no place. Dogs do not act out of spite. Here are some possible reasons for your dog's demolition of your couch, floor, favorite shoes, or whatever:

- *Boredom:* One of the ways dogs relieve boredom is by chewing. They will chew whatever is available to them or what they enjoy most. Think of how much fun it must be to rip the stuffing out of a couch and watch it fly all over the living room!
- *Fun:* No explanation necessary.
- *Tension:* Dogs, unlike people, don't keep tension bottled up. They release it, usually by chewing. If your departure upsets your

dog, for instance, he may chew the kitchen table leg to relieve his anxiety.

- *Lack of exercise:* All dogs need exercise and some need more than others. If your dog does not get enough exercise, he may use chewing as an outlet for his pent-up energy.

- *Poor diet or hunger tension:* Dogs that are not getting proper nutrition or that are sensitive to food additives may exhibit any number of behavior problems, like chewing.

- *Teething:* When puppies lose their milk teeth (baby teeth), they need to chew on things much the way human babies do when they cut teeth. After the adult teeth are all in, when your pup is about six months old, the teeth will begin to set in the jaw. At this time, puppies need to chew more than ever. If your puppy is between 6-10 months old and is left in an empty room, he will chew the walls and floor because he has to chew.

"He Has Plenty of Chew Toys But He Still Chews My Things."

If your dog has many chew toys on the floor it will be harder for him to differentiate between what's his and what's yours. It all looks like fair game to him. If, however, he has just one or two toys, it is much easier to teach him the difference. When he is better trained you may wish to add a couple more. It is also a good idea to reserve one favorite toy that your dog only gets when you are gone. It will become a special treat that will occupy more of his time than his ordinary, everyday toys.

Dogs become demolition experts because of boredom, tension, poor diet, or lack of exercise.

"He Knows He's Done Wrong. He Looks Guilty When I Get Home."

Dogs don't have morals and don't know right from wrong. When your dog looks "guilty" he is actually saying, in dog language, that he is submissive and/or scared. He is in effect saying, "I respect you and don't want you to hurt me." Let's consider what leads up to that guilty look: You leave for work and for some reason, perhaps boredom, your dog begins to chew a shoe you forgot to put away. It feels good on his gums and the leather tastes especially nice. He flips it in the air a few times for laughs. Eventually, he loses interest and takes a nap.

A few hours later you come home. Your dog is happy to see you and you him—until you find the rest of what used to be your shoe. So you yell and maybe even hit him as you show him the chewed shoe. On another day you leave for work and your dog discovers how much fun it is to rip the stuffing out of the couch cushions. He has a real blast scattering that puffy white stuff all over the living room. Some time later you arrive home to find this mess and again let your dog know how unhappy you are.

Notice a pattern? Your dog has. He knows that he has a great time when he chews up your things and that he has a really bad time when you come home. Your dog has not learned that chewing is bad. He has fun when he chews. What he has learned is that your homecoming is very unpleasant. So now, after a great day's chewing, when he hears you drive into the driveway, he gets scared and submissive and looks guilty. He reacts this way because he knows he'll be punished when you walk in the door, not because he knows he has done something wrong. To teach your dog not to chew something, you need to catch him in or before the act. When he so much as looks at your shoe or the couch or whatever, utter a sharp, bark-like sound and/or clap your hands to startle your dog and interrupt his actions or thoughts. Then give him something else to do like chew on his own toy, come to you, or sit on command. Punishing him after the fact will do nothing more than confuse him and damage your relationship with him.

"He Only Chews Things When I'm Not There to Catch Him."

When you are away from home or are too busy to watch your dog, confine him in a place where he can't get into trouble. For some dogs, this can be a small room. For many, this means a dog crate. When confined, your dog will be safe and will not be able to get into anything he shouldn't. When you confine him, make sure he has fresh water and a safe chew toy. A stuffed Kong is great for confinement. When you come home at the end of the day, it will be with the comfort of knowing that your house is in one piece and you and your dog will both be happy to see each other. If your dog has already developed a habit of chewing your things, you may need to crate him for a long time before the habit is broken. When you begin to give him more freedom, do so gradually to help prevent setbacks. If you have a puppy, plan to crate him until he is at least one year old to get through the worst of the teething periods.

It will also be helpful to your dog if you make your departure and homecoming low-key and uneventful. If you get your dog excited just before you leave, he will be more anxious about your going. The same holds true for your return. If your greeting is a very excited one, your dog will begin to get revved up around the time you usually get home. If you are late, your dog will need to do something to relieve his anxiety and pent-up energy. He will chew. Similarly, if you always feed your dog or take him out to relieve himself immediately upon arriving home, your dog will learn to get excited around the time you are due back. Get your dog used to the pattern that your homecoming means a quiet "Hello" and a pat on the head, and that going out and eating have no connection with your return. Let your dog out 10-15 minutes after you arrive (with the exception of a young pup who has been confined for an extended period of time) and feed him 30 minutes to an hour after that.

"What Else Can I Do?"

Give your dog lots of physical and mental exercise to provide him with constructive ways to release his energy. Along with one to two hours of physical exercise a day, give your dog a mental workout in the form of training. Training gives your dog a job to do and you will strengthen your relationship with him by establishing clear (and fun) communication. Feed your dog a high-quality, naturally formulated dog food to ensure that your dog is not being destructive because of a nutritional imbalance or sensitivity to additives in his diet. Feed adult dogs twice a day and young puppies three to four times. Give your dog every chance to behave his very best.

Daycare may be another good option for your dog. At a good daycare dogs will be active for part of the day and have nap breaks between their play sessions. If you cannot afford daycare every day, even a day or two a week can make a big difference.

"My Dog Doesn't Eat the Couch Anymore!"

By trying to understand your dog and his behavior and by following a common sense approach, you'll be well on your way to having a dog that is a joy to live with, a couch (and carpet and walls and shoes) that is intact, and a lifetime of friendship with your dog.

Pulling... Whoa!

Well-mannered dogs don't drag their owners down the street. Along with jumping up on people, pulling is perhaps the number one complaint owners have with their dogs. For puppies, the solution is to never let them acquire the pulling habit in the first place. Dogs pull on lead because they have been inadvertently rewarded for pulling. Dogs and puppies pull to get to something they want; anyone who has ever held a child's hand while visiting an amusement park knows this feeling! What you need to teach your dog is that the way to get what he wants is not to pull on the lead, but to remain at your side.

Tugging engages the opposition reflex: the dog instinctively pulls back against pressure. When you pull on the leash, the same thing happens—you encourage the dog to pull against you.

Indoors, teach your dog to follow alongside you by having him follow a toy or a food lure (held in your hand) at your side. Click and reward when he is walking nicely at your side. After he is following you everywhere, back and forth in the house, put on a lead and just stand there. When your dog is focused on you and not fussing with the lead, click and reward him. Now play the follow-me game with your dog dragging the lead, once again rewarding your dog when he is at your side. Now pick up the lead and, making sure it is loose at all times, continue to play and reward the follow-me game.

Repeat the same process outside in the yard. There are distractions about, so be ready for a setback or two. But remember, no pulling by either one of you! Dogs have an opposition reflex; you pull, he pulls, and so it continues.

One reason so many dogs become dedicated pullers is that when the leash is tight and they are pulling into it, they know exactly where we are (at the other end of the leash). So they can ignore us and focus on other things in the environment. When the leash is loose, they are not so sure where we are, so they have to check in to see what we are up to. Keeping the leash loose and rewarding all good walking behavior is a great way to have your dog pay better attention to you!

No one in the family should ever be allowed to walk your dog on leash if your dog is pulling that person. It's not safe for either your dog or the person. Children are particularly at risk, so close supervision is required. It's not cute that your dog drags the kids or that the kids drag your dog; it's just plain dangerous.

When first heading outside, it is important to give your dog some slack in the leash and let him sniff and explore his environment (remember: keep that lead loose). Allowing your dog to explore for a moment or two is critical in teaching dogs not to pull. Owners constantly pulling on dogs only adds to the spiraling pulling problem. Let him sniff a bit, and then practice your loose-lead walking. Use a reasonable length leash when training, at least 5' and perhaps a bit longer. Avoid the extremes of a lead that's too short or too long at this stage.

When your dog starts to pull, just stay in place and wait for him to stop. Once he does, click/reward the loose lead and continue on your way. There are various harnesses and head collars that can be helpful to manage pulling while you are teaching a loose-leash walking behavior.

PART 4 # General Dog Ownership Tips

Leash Training

If your puppy has never been on a leash, we recommend that you get him used to being on a leash before the first night if you are attending class. Follow the directions below and contact a professional if you have any questions.

Put a plain buckle-type collar on your puppy and let him become used to having something around his neck. Do this when you are around to watch to make sure that the puppy does not get his collar caught on anything. Always remove the collar when you are not home to avoid the possibility of accidental strangulation.

Once the puppy is comfortable with the collar, attach a lightweight leash and let the puppy drag it around where it will not get caught on anything. Do this until the puppy is ignoring the leash. Never leave the puppy unattended with the leash on; always be attentive. The next step is to pick up the leash and follow the puppy around without any tension on the leash. The final step is to encourage your puppy to follow you. In a happy tone, use your voice to encourage your puppy to

Entice your dog to follow you by dragging a toy on the ground.

walk toward you. If your puppy does not respond, try to use food or a toy to entice him to follow. Be sure to use plenty of praise when your puppy is walking along with you. Remember, never drag or pull your puppy; this will only make the process take longer. Take your time, be patient, and praise.

Housetraining Tips

Because most people embarking on the adventure of housetraining will be doing so with a puppy, most of the information in this guide relates directly to puppies, but all the principles can be successfully applied to adult dogs as well.

Have a Plan

Since housetraining is probably the first thing you will teach your dog, it is important that the method you choose be one that instills a basis for trust and understanding. Housetraining does not need to be traumatic for you or your dog. What housetraining requires is persistence combined with a little knowledge. To make the process go smoothly, keep in mind some basic principles:

- Your dog is instinctively a clean animal.
- Your dog will be happy to follow your rules as long as he understands what they are.
- Your dog does not soil the house out of spite or to "get even" with you. Your dog soils the house for one of two reasons: either he doesn't understand that he shouldn't or he doesn't have the necessary control not to.

If you keep these principles in mind, your housetraining program can be divided into three parts:

- Taking advantage of your dog's instinct to be clean
- Giving him clear-cut rules
- Making it as easy as possible for him to succeed

Take Advantage of Your Dog's Instinct to Be Clean

Most dogs will not soil their living/sleeping quarters, so use this instinct to your best advantage. When you can't watch your dog, confine him to a small area or a crate. A crate is a cage or travel-type kennel that serves as a sort of playpen and bed for your dog. It is a place where he can be safe, secure, and out of trouble when you aren't able to supervise him. The crate should be just big enough for your dog to be able to stand, turn around, and lie down. Too much room will give him enough space to sleep in one end and soil the other. For best results, get your dog used to his new "room" gradually, using food or a toy to encourage him to go into it. Once your dog is used to going into the crate, slowly increase the length of time you leave him in it with the door closed. Continue to give him a food reward every time he goes into the crate.

Most dogs like having the den-like security a crate provides. Adult dogs can be left in a crate for up to eight hours if necessary. Puppies, of course, need to eliminate much more often than adults. Puppies under three or four months of age have very little bladder and bowel control and should not be left in a crate for more than a couple of hours. As their control improves they can be confined for up to four to six hours at a time. Most puppies and dogs can sleep through the night in a crate because their body's metabolism slows down.

Give Your Dog Clear-Cut Rules

- Dogs are not born knowing what we want. We must teach them our rules in a manner they can understand. Dogs understand absolutes: black and white, yes and no, pleasant and unpleasant. There are two absolutes in housetraining: eliminating outside is good and eliminating in the house is not.
- Teach your dog where to go. Choose an area of your yard to serve as your dog's "bathroom." Take him there often, on leash, and wait for him to go. As soon as your dog goes to the bathroom, praise him and give him a reward. A piece of food or a toy usually works for most dogs. Teach him that the first order of business when he goes outside is to go to the bathroom. Always take him to his bathroom area first, then play with him or take him for a walk.
- Teach your dog where *not* to go. If you catch your dog going to the bathroom in the house, utter a sharp "Stop" or make some other startling noise to get him to stop. Immediately take him to his bathroom area and wait for him to go. Then praise and reward him. If you do not catch him in the act, *do not scold him!* Do not yell at him, drag him to the mess, or rub his nose in it. He will not make the connection between your anger and his having gone to the bathroom earlier. Just clean up the mess and keep a closer watch on your dog next time. Use white vinegar and water for cleaning. It neutralizes the odor and will discourage your dog from going back to that spot.

Make It Easy for Your Dog to Succeed

- *Set a schedule.* Take your dog out on a regular schedule—every hour or so for young puppies—and stick to that schedule, even on the weekends. Feed your dog on a regular schedule to help regulate his system. Puppies need to be fed three to four times a day and adult dogs twice daily. Regular feeding will enable you to know when your dog will probably need to go out.

- *Be alert.* Keep a close eye on your dog. Watch for cues that he needs to go out. Circling and sniffing are strong indications that your puppy needs to go out. There are other times that your puppy will need to be taken to his bathroom area. He will need to go out after waking up (even from a short nap), after playing, after he has been confined, and after eating or drinking.

- *Use a crate.* When you can't watch your dog, keep him in his crate. If he has been confined for a while, take your dog to his bathroom area before giving him freedom in the house or yard. If he does not go to the bathroom, put him back in his crate for a while and try again later. The fewer mistakes your dog makes, the faster he will become housetrained.

- *Feed a high-quality diet.* Many dog foods have excess salt, sugar, and fillers that can interfere with housetraining efforts. If your dog is consuming a lot of salt, he will drink more and therefore have to urinate more. If he is getting too much bulk in his diet, he will have to move his bowels much more frequently. Stick to a high-quality, naturally preserved, premium dog food. You will find these foods primarily in pet stores.

- *Monitor water intake.* Give your dog lots of water in his food so he will be less likely to drink between meals. Always have water available, though, especially in hot weather. With young puppies it is a good idea to pick up water two or three hours before bedtime to enable them to sleep through the night without having to go out.

- *Make sure your dog is healthy.* If you have followed the above guidelines and your dog appears to have no control at all or seems to have to eliminate more than you think is normal, he may have a problem like worms or a bladder infection. It is best to be safe. If you suspect your dog has a problem, seek veterinary help.

Learning Takes Time!

There will be days when your puppy seems to be getting the idea and others when it feels like all your efforts have been in vain. *Don't be discouraged!* This is a normal part of the learning process. Your dog may even do well for several months and then have a setback. This is a normal part of housetraining. Remember that dogs are individuals and learn at different rates. If you take one step at a time and keep in mind how your dog learns, it won't be long before you have a house-trained dog!

Crate Training

A crate can be a beneficial training tool for you and your dog.

What Is a Crate?

A crate is a room for your dog—a place where he can be safe and secure (and out of trouble) when you can't watch him. Crates come in three basic styles: plastic (airline-type), collapsible wire, and custom-made steel. All three have advantages and disadvantages depending on your particular needs.

A crate is a dog's safe and comfortable den.
Dogs get used to and like having a crate.

Will My Dog Like Being in a Crate?

Because dogs are instinctively den animals, they get used to and actually like having a crate. You may have noticed that when your dog is frightened or doesn't feel well, he seeks out a closed-in space, like under the coffee table, behind the couch, or under the bed. A crate serves as your dog's room—his own place of security.

Why Should I Use a Crate?

Crates are useful in a number of ways. They can be used for training, for traveling, and for confinement when you are unable to supervise.

- *Puppy training:* Use the crate for housetraining. Because dogs don't like to soil where they sleep, you can confine your dog to the crate to prevent accidents when you can't supervise. Use the crate to prevent destructive chewing. All puppies chew; they chew when they are teething, when they are bored, when they are in need of exercise, and just because they like to chew.
- *Traveling:* A crate-trained dog can travel with you because you can always bring his "room" along! If your dog ever has to travel on an airplane where he must be crated, it will be much easier if he is already used to a crate. A crate is also the safest place for your dog to be when riding in the car.
- *Problem solving:* A crate can help solve behavior problems such as destructive chewing or separation anxiety. In a crate, your dog will feel secure and cannot get into trouble.

How Big Should the Crate Be?

The crate should be big enough for your dog to be able to stand up, lie down, and turn around. Puppies should have this much room and no more. Given too much room, they may soil at one end and sleep in the other. When you buy a crate for your puppy, you may want to buy the size he'll need as an adult and block off the excess space. Give him more space as he grows and becomes housetrained. Many animal shelters, veterinarians, and pet stores rent crates.

How Do I Get My Dog Used to the Crate?

The crate should represent something positive to your dog, so begin with a happy voice and lots of food. With the crate door open and secured in place, throw a piece of food or a toy in the crate as you verbally encourage your dog to go in. Many people like to give their dog a cue like *Go to Bed, Kennel,* or *Go in Your House.* Whatever you choose, be consistent and your dog will catch on quickly. Once your dog is used to going into the crate to get the food, begin shutting the door behind him. Tell him to get in, throw the food in, and shut the door. Make sure to praise him every time he goes into the crate. Gradually increase the length of time he stays in the crate with the door closed. Once he is comfortable staying in the crate for several minutes, begin to leave the room for short periods. Then increase the length of time from there. To speed up the process, feed your dog his meals in the crate. Always make sure going into the crate is a positive experience for your dog.

What If My Dog Barks in His Crate?

Sometimes dogs will bark out of protest, boredom, or loneliness. It is very important to never let your dog out of his crate when he is barking or whining! If you do, he will learn very quickly that this is the key to being let out of the crate. If your dog barks or whines in the crate, ignore him unless you feel he needs to go out to eliminate. Only let him out when he is quiet, even if just for a second or two. If your dog sleeps in the crate, have it in your bedroom or nearby. Dogs are social animals and don't like to be isolated. He will be less likely to bark out of loneliness if he is near you. This is especially true for young puppies.

How Long Can I Leave My Dog in the Crate?

Puppies under three months of age can be crated for an hour or two; older pups can be confined for three to four hours. When absolutely necessary, adult dogs can stay in a crate for up to eight hours at a time, provided they are otherwise given ample exercise and attention. Always make sure your dog has had a chance to relieve himself before being crated for an extended period of time. In my opinion, dogs should not be crated for extended periods of time on a regular basis (beyond sleeping at night).

Will I Have to Use the Crate Forever?

When used properly, in conjunction with basic training, the crate can eventually become just an option for most dogs and their owners. You will probably find, however, that it is a very handy thing to have around well after your dog is trained. Some dogs will always need to be confined when left alone. Every dog is different and common sense will tell you if and when your dog can be left unattended in the house.

Guidelines for Life with Your Dog

Dogs are opportunists and learn quickly how to get what they want. That may be attention from you or food on the counter: if they try something and it works, they will try again and again for the possibility of random reinforcement. This is why it is important to adhere to consistent rules. Consistency is the key to how your dog will learn what works and what doesn't work to get treats, attention, or whatever he may want or need. You can shape your dog's everyday behavior by being aware of what you are reinforcing every time you interact with your dog. Sound like a lot of work? Yes, but well worth the commitment to have a well-behaved dog that can be part of society and your life. Dominant behaviors include: guarding food, begging, growling, biting, and demanding attention, petting, food, or toys. Tune in to signs of pushy behavior and turn the tables in a positive manner with training and consistent management so your dog understands what is expected. Here are some suggestions:

- Train your dog, and use your training in daily life with your dog. By teaching him to respond to your cues, you are showing him that you make the rules, what those rules are, and that he must adhere to them.

- Teach your dog to have a place that means lie down and relax, such as a particular mat. Teaching your dog to lie down on cue puts you in better control of his behavior.

- Make sure you go first everywhere or give your dog permission to go—that is your privilege and good doggy manners. Train your dog to wait at doorways and stairways while you go first. Then tell him when he may proceed. Also teach your dog that you have the right of way; train your dog to move out of the way.

- Make your dog earn all petting and treats. If he nudges you or barks at you for attention, petting, or food, ignore him. Only pet him or feed him if he earns it by responding to a cue. *No unearned petting, food, treats, or hugs!* You control the resources. Teach tricks for treats and attention!

- If you have any control problems, discontinue all roughhousing and tug games. Tug can teach your dog to use his physical strength against you. (And probably win. After all, who usually quits first?) Teach him to fetch. In this game, he works for you. Tug is okay once you have a reliable *Give* cue, so you can be the one who ends the game *every* time. Use tugging to your advantage. Assuming there are no prior possession or aggression issues, tug is a great way to burn off excess energy or to use as the ultimate reward for some dogs.

- Have your dog sleep in his own bed—not yours. Leaders get the best sleeping place. If your dog is permitted on the furniture, allow him to join you by invitation only. If he is on the couch you want to sit on, have him get off before you sit and then wait to be invited back up.

- Give your dog two or three toys at a time to help him understand that everything else belongs to you. Have more toys to rotate through to keep interest high.
- Discourage all jumping up, paws on your shoulders, and cuddles in your lap except by invitation only. Having your dog on you or higher than you can be a strong message that he is in control.
- Stop all mouthing and biting—even in play.

Whether you want a perfect pet or perfect competition dog, following these basic guidelines will help improve your relationship and prevent behavior problems. If you have questions about a behavior please seek help for special assistance in addition to following these guidelines.

Note: Being in charge doesn't mean you and your dog can't be friends; it just means that for the sake of your dog's safety and your relationship with him, you have to be the one who makes the decisions. You need to be able to uphold the rules so you can take care of your dog in a responsible manner. You are responsible for your dog and his behavior, not the other way around. These steps can help achieve a balanced and harmonious relationship.

PART 5

Resources

The Benefits of Neutering Your Dog

Contributed by Dr. Spodick of Swan Corner Animal Hospital

Most people understand the necessity for population control, but not too many understand the unique benefits that neutering a male dog can provide. Often, owners of male dogs are nervous that neutering the dog will change his personality and turn him into a different dog. This is not at all true. Neutering dogs does tend to take the edge off of an unusually aggressive dog, and it does decrease roaming and marking behaviors. But most owners consider a change in these behaviors to be a positive change. And while those behaviors are eliminated or minimized, the male dog's essential personality remains completely unchanged.

Neutering also provides numerous medical benefits. In every unneutered male dog, the prostate gland begins to enlarge measurably by five to six years of age. An enlarged prostate gland is prone to cancerous tumors, cysts, and infection. Even if the prostate does not develop any of these problems, soon after it starts to enlarge, it starts to interfere with the male dog's ability to defecate and urinate properly. Dogs that have been neutered have small prostate glands that do not develop any problems. And in fact, if a dog does develop prostate problems, the first course of action is to neuter him, which is a risky proposition if the dog is 9 to 10 years old at the time.

Unneutered male dogs are also more prone to cancerous tumors of the testicles and perianal glands. The development of these tumors can be directly traced to testosterone, which is the primary hormone released by the testicles. Testosterone also seems to be linked to the development of a special type of hernia in the anal region. This hernia often requires extensive, expensive surgical repair.

Neutering male dogs at a young age protects them from the development of all the problems mentioned above and will prolong their lives in a number of ways. It will also make your male dog a better companion for his entire life.

The Benefits of Spaying Your Dog

Contributed by Dr. Spodick of Swan Corner Animal Hospital

For female dogs, the benefits of spaying have been crystal clear for a number of years. Often, people resist spaying their female dogs and even want their female dog to have "just one litter, to make them a better pet." This old wives' tale is entirely untrue. There is no evidence that supports the notion that whelping a litter improves the temperament of a female dog, and there is substantial evidence that allowing a female dog to even go through one heat cycle can predispose her to many medical problems, including cancer.

Every time a female dog goes through a heat cycle, her body (whether she is mated or not) reacts as if it is actually pregnant. This change can be very subtle or it can be pronounced. Some female dogs will gain weight, make milk, and even go into "labor," even though they have no puppies to give birth to. This phenomenon is called pseudopregnancy, and in female dogs, it is universal, although behavioral signs may not manifest.

When a female dog goes through pseudopregnancy, her uterus swells and fills with fluid to prepare to nurture the puppies. After the pseudopregnancy ends, most (but not all) of the fluid drains away. Over subsequent heats, the volume of fluid in the uterus steadily increases. A uterus that has fluid in it is predisposed to an infection called pyometra, which can cause kidney failure, shock, and even death. In unspayed female dogs, pyometra is so common that it is not a matter of if it will happen, but when. The treatment for pyometra is an emergency surgery to spay the dog, which once again is a very risky procedure, because a dog with this infection is always in critical condition when it is diagnosed. Many dogs with pyometra die during surgery or shortly thereafter, despite the best efforts of veterinary professionals.

Another change that female dogs experience during pseudopregnancy is the development of their mammary glands to produce milk. As dogs go through successive heats, this repeated stimulation dramatically increases their risk of breast cancer. Breast cancer in dogs is as deadly as it is in people. Radiation therapy and chemotherapy usually do not touch the cancer once it has occurred, and only radical surgery early on can possibly cure it. Studies have shown that after only one heat cycle, a dog's chances of contracting breast cancer goes up 35% to 40%. Because of this, it is important to spay your dog, and you should seriously consider spaying her before she even goes through her first heat cycle (usually at 7 to 9 months of age).

Female dogs that have been spayed at an early age almost never suffer from these life-threatening infections and cancerous tumors. Taking action when your dog is young can make a tremendous impact on her long-term survival, prolonging her life and making her a better companion for years to come.

What You Should Know About Feeding Your Dog

One thing we all have in common is that each day, we feed our dogs. When it comes to pets, there certainly seems to be a link between their behaviors and their diets. We have all heard the expression, "You are what you eat," and it seems logical to apply this approach when feeding our dogs. Educators have always stressed that good-quality nutrition plays an important role in childhood learning. It just makes sense that diet quality can have an effect on how our dogs behave and learn as well.

A high-quality diet of either fresh/frozen or canned/dry with a minimum of natural preservatives seems to be our best bet. Look at the label; you should find several high-quality protein sources in the first few ingredients. Ingredients are listed in order of their content in the food. If grains make up the majority of the first six ingredients, then you're mainly getting grain for your dog food dollar.

It seems that the country you live in has a great deal to do with what the dog population gets fed. In the U.S., we have lots of corn and wheat so this is what tends to get into our commercial pet foods. In Europe, there is little or no corn and beef so other grains and meats get used. Japan uses a lot of fish and, yes, dogs in Australia do get emu, kangaroo, and rabbit in their diets. A certain amount of whole grains in dog food is an excellent idea, but too much and you're just not giving your dog what he needs. Dogs are primarily carnivores.

Read the Bag

The front of the bag is usually advertising, so the side panel or the back of the bag is often where the important information is found. Let's take a look.

Know what your dog is eating and select his food carefully.

Interpreting the AAFCO Statement

What you're looking for here is that the food has been tested in the Association of American Feed Control Officials (AAFCO) feeding trials and that it fulfills certain basic nutritional requirements. Note that the AAFCO statement only applies to commercially prepared foods, but that is what most owners tend to feed. AAFCO classifications include:

- *Correct for all life stages:* This means that the food will support both the growth of young dogs and adult maintenance. Puppies and/or adult dogs could be fed this diet.
- *Adult maintenance:* This means it's okay for adult dogs, but for your new puppy you need to make another choice.
- *Growth:* Okay for puppies but perhaps too much for adult dogs.

When to shift from growth to adult? Check with your veterinarian but most dogs can make this change at about six to nine months of age.

Product names don't always give us the correct information, so make sure you read the label. If a dog food is labeled as a "chicken and rice formula" then its first two ingredients should be chicken and rice. Sources like beef, fish, pork, poultry, and eggs are high-quality sources and supply important amino acids. It's sad to say that most diets found in the superstores and grocery stores just don't meet these criteria. These diets tend to be grain-based and because manufacturers are looking for maximum shelf life and little or no spoilage, they also tend to be heavy on the preservatives. Grain-heavy foods are carbohydrate-rich and since carbohydrates convert to sugars in the body, you may see weight problems and hyperactivity. Protein resources in supermarket diets tend to be of lower quality as well.

Preservatives can give dogs problems. Some of these chemical preservatives can influence both your dog's health and behavior. Try to avoid foods that use BHA, BHT, or ethoxyquin as preservatives. Rather, look for brands that use vitamin C and vitamin E, which is often listed as "mixed tocopherols." Also, be on the lookout for artificial colors; these chemical dyes are used to make the food look good to us and they offer your dog nothing in the way of enhanced nutrition.

Fresh-frozen diets do not require preservatives but do require proper refrigeration. Once thawed, they must be stored and handled properly and must be consumed within a few days of thawing.

A Word on Feeding Raw Diets

Many owners are successfully feeding a "raw" diet to mimic a natural carnivore diet. It is important that you educate yourself before taking on this endeavor to be sure that you provide a balanced diet. Done properly, a raw diet can be accomplished quite easily with great results. For more information check out these titles:

- *Holistic Guide For A Healthy Dog* by Wendy Volhard
- *Give Your Dog A Bone* by Dr. Ian Billinghurst
- *The Ultimate Diet* by Kymythy Schultze

Exercise

Dogs on super-high carbohydrate diets or older dogs that are still on puppy food and don't get enough exercise can exhibit problem behaviors such as destructive behavior or hyperactivity. Make sure that you match your dog's diet to his lifestyle and go for a walk or play with your dog as often as you can.

So, What Should I Feed?

You have other options but because these diets are not produced and marketed by mega-corporations, you may not have even heard of some of these foods. It's confusing to think that if the ABC Dog Food Company really knows how to make a quality dog food and wants you to have the best nutrition for your dog, why do they then make and market 30 different types of dog food? It seems that they are making things harder for the average dog owner to select a diet by providing too many similar choices.

A diet change is not a magic potion, but a healthy dog goes to the vet less for chronic illness and often is better behaved and just plain looks healthier. Your dog may be on a special diet because of health reasons. If this is true for your pet, you should always speak with your vet before contemplating any diet change. Plenty of fresh, clean drinking water should always be available.

You can usually feed less of a premium natural diet so the cost per feeding is about the same or perhaps even less than you are currently spending. High-quality diets tend to be more digestible so you clean up less waste. If all your dog's food seems to go directly from the bowl to your yard, your dog may not be getting the nutrition he needs. Dogs should have one or two well-formed bowel movements each day. Many more than that and your dog may not be getting the best nutrition from his current diet.

If you change your dog's diet, change about 20% of the food each day for five days. Be on the lookout for any health problems. If you have changed your dog over to a natural diet, congratulations! Now make sure that the treats you use are also of a high quality. Give the new diet about 8 to 12 weeks and then see if you notice improvement in your pet's overall health and behavior.

Doggie Daycare

Daycare is one of the best inventions of the late 20th century! It's a guilt-free solution to long workdays, which leave your companion home alone. Not enough time to exercise your dog? Does your dog have separation anxiety? Are you looking for a place to get some socialization for your pup? Daycare is for you! Check out facilities carefully, and be sure to get references.

Choosing the Right Person to Watch Over Your Pup

In the past, pet owners had very few choices concerning care for their animals while they were away. In looking for new alternatives, you now have several options:

Doggie daycare burns off energy and socializes your dog with others.

- *Dog walkers:* Visit your pet in your own home for a specific period of time each day.
- *Pet sitters:* Stay overnight with your pet in your own home.
- *Boarders:* Provide overnight and daytime accommodations for your pet in a home environment.
- *Kennels:* Provide overnight and daytime accommodations for your pet in a kennel environment.

So how do you choose which one is right for you? The choice is largely up to your preference. Here are some tips to help you choose the right person to watch over your pup:

- Ask fellow owners or your trainer, veterinarian, groomer, or pet-supply store for referrals.
- Price ranges vary with location.

If choosing a dog walker or pet sitter:

- Is she bonded? Does she carry commercial liability insurance?
- Is she a member of a professional association?
- How long has she been in business?
- Does she provide references?
- Does she provide a service contract?
- What is her training? How extensive is her knowledge of medical concerns? Has she taken pet-healthcare seminars or had any training through a pet sitters' group, local humane society, or other organization?

Once you have narrowed down the options and are deciding on the right person to watch over your dog:

Have her meet your pet in advance, and watch how she interacts with your pet.

Expect questions. She should ask about your animal's eating habits, toilet habits, grooming needs, exercise routines, and medications. She should also ask for telephone numbers.

Once the decision is made:

- Make reservations, the earlier the better.
- Confirming the reservations before you leave is essential.
- Provide detailed but simple instructions in writing. Leave a measuring cup, for instance, and say exactly how much your pup should be fed. (A "handful" or "bowlful" does not mean the same thing to everyone.)
- Always leave a telephone number where you can be reached and the number of your veterinarian. Call if you plan to return early or late.

Dog Walkers

From strapping a leash on for a good old-fashioned walk to a good "tire him out" romp or game of ball in your yard, a dog walker's time is dedicated to fulfilling the program that they create for your dog. Most of them can also feed, brush, clip toenails, administer most medications, or just cuddle and kiss your dog. A great solution for your dog that is home alone for long periods of time. Dog walkers are great for puppies and housetraining.

Pet Sitters

Each day that you are away, your pet sitter will be responsible for both your pet and your home, so it is important to choose a pet sitter carefully. Here are some tips from the National Association of Professional Pet Sitters (NAPPS) and other pros:

- Does your dog walker or pet sitter have a plan if she is unable to make it to your house?
- Have your own contingency plan, especially in the North come winter. Provide the pet sitter with the name of someone, maybe a neighbor, who can take care of your pet should weather, for example, prevent the sitter from getting there.
- Have plenty of supplies on hand—food, needed medications, and grooming implements.
- Inform the sitter of your pet's special habits—favorite hiding places, for example, or phobias.

Boarders

When your pet can't be with you, you can send him to the home of a trusted pet-care provider. In many ways, this option is better for you and your pet. Although your dog is in a new environment, he has his own crate, mat, food and water dish, toys, and so on, and you don't have the extra worry of someone else staying in your home while you are away.

Kennels

Of course, the traditional kennel is always an option. When choosing a kennel, be sure to ask for a tour of the facility. If they won't let you see where your dog will be staying, don't leave your pet there! Inspect it personally, talk to your veterinarian and all the other dog people you know to hear of their experiences with that kennel, and also look for certain practices. Are all dogs required to be vaccinated—including against kennel cough? Will your dog get his regular food, and any medications? Find out if someone will be present 24 hours a day. Some kennels will even provide the option of paying for extra playtime and walks.

Bibliography

Don't Shoot the Dog, Karen Pryor
How To Raise A Puppy You Can Live With, Clarice Rutherford and
    David H. Neil
Culture Clash, Jean Donaldson
Dog Language: An Encyclopedia of Canine Behavior,
    Roger Abrantes
The Evolution of Canine Social Behavior, Roger Abrantes
*Excel-erated Learning: Explaining in Plain English How Dogs
    Learn and How Best to Teach Them,* Pamela J. Reid, Ph.D.
How Dogs Learn, Mary R. Burch, Ph.D. and Jon S. Bailey, Ph.D.
Readings in Companion Animal Behavior, Peter L. Borchelt and
    Victoria L. Voith
Behavior Problems in Dogs, William E. Campbell
Behavior Booklets, Ian Dunbar and Gwen Bohnenkamp
Second-Hand Dog, Carol Benjamin
What All Good Dogs Should Know: The Sensible Way to Train,
    Jack Volhard and Melissa Bartlett

Childproofing Your Dog: A Complete Guide to Preparing Your Dog for the Children in Your Life, Brian Kilcommons and Sarah Wilson

Gettng Started: Clicker Training for Dogs, Karen Pryor

Clicker Training for Obedience, Morgan Spector

Beyond Basic Dog Training, Diane L. Bauman

Teaching Dog Obedience Classes: The Manual for Instructors, Joachim Volhard, Gail Tamases Fisher, and Job Evans

Training Your Dog: The Step-by-Step Manual, Joachim Volhard and Gail Tamases Fisher

Holistic Guide for a Healthy Dog, Wendy Volhard and Kerry Brown

Give Your Dog A Bone, Ian Billinghurst

Dr. Pitcairn's Complete Guide to Natural Health for Dogs and Cats, Richard H. Pitcairn, D.V.M, Ph.D. and Susan Hubble Pitcairn

The New Knowledge of Dog Behavior, Clarence Pfaffenberger

Gary Wilkes Behavior Sampler, Gary Wilkes

On Talking Terms with Dogs, Turid Rugaas

Acknowledgements

There are so many to acknowledge but I will begin with those that bring us all together. The dogs—all the dogs that have touched my life have a part in this book, and with them their people.

The information in this work has come from many years of interacting with dogs and their people and teaching others to teach people and their dogs. I thank all of those who have been a part of this project, especially the Gemini Dog Training staff who helped with the program development and editing the first drafts, in particular Paul Emerson, Jean McCord, Barbara (Hickcox)Van Raden, and Michelle Borelli.

Also of great importance to my ability to get the project completed are those who put up with my long hours; my husband Chuck and my mom, thanks for the patience and dinners. My ever-faithful friend Dana Crevling, who is always there to listen to my ideas, pushes when I need it, and has been instrumental in opening many doors for me along the way.

And finally a big thank you to Monica Percival for trying something a little different and to the editing staff at Clean Run, who have guided me through this project.